INTERNATIONAL PERSPECTIVE
IN CRITICISM
∙∙

GOETHE · GRILLPARZER
SAINTE-BEUVE · LOWELL

JAMES RUSSELL LOWELL

INTERNATIONAL PERSPECTIVE IN CRITICISM

∴

GOETHE · GRILLPARZER
SAINTE-BEUVE · LOWELL

By

GUSTAV POLLAK

KENNIKAT PRESS, INC./PORT WASHINGTON, N. Y.

PREFATORY NOTE

The author's thanks are due to the Houghton
Mifflin Company, Boston, for courteous permission to use the extracts from Lowell contained in
this volume. The translations from and concerning Goethe, Grillparzer and Sainte-Beuve are the
author's own. The passages reprinted from his
book on *Franz Grillparzer and the Austrian
Drama* are marked by an asterisk (*).

INTERNATIONAL PERSPECTIVE IN CRITICISM

Copyright 1914 by Gustav Pollak
Reissued in 1965 by Kennikat Press

Library of Congress Catalog Card No: 65-18610

CONTENTS

PAGE

INTRODUCTION xiii

GOETHE'S UNIVERSAL INTERESTS 1

GRILLPARZER'S ORIGINALITY AS CRITIC 24

SAINTE-BEUVE'S UNIQUE PLACE IN LITERATURE . 39

LOWELL, PATRIOT AND COSMOPOLITAN 58

GOETHE, GRILLPARZER, SAINTE-BEUVE AND LOWELL
    ON COMMON GROUND 85

  ENGLISH LITERATURE

    GOETHE ON MELANCHOLY IN ENGLISH POETS . . 87
    GOETHE ON GOLDSMITH 93
    GOETHE ON WALTER SCOTT 94
    GRILLPARZER ON WALTER SCOTT 95
    LOWELL ON WALTER SCOTT 97
    GOETHE ON BYRON 98
    GRILLPARZER ON BYRON 99
    LOWELL ON BYRON 101
    SAINTE-BEUVE ON LORD CHESTERFIELD 102
    GOETHE ON SHAKESPEARE 106
    GRILLPARZER ON SHAKESPEARE 110
    LOWELL ON SHAKESPEARE 122

  FRENCH LITERATURE

    GOETHE ON VOLTAIRE 136
    GOETHE ON MADAME DE STAËL 139
    GRILLPARZER ON MADAME DE STAËL 143
    GOETHE ON MOLIÈRE 145
    GRILLPARZER ON MOLIÈRE 147
    SAINTE-BEUVE ON MOLIÈRE 149
    GOETHE ON BÉRANGER 168
    SAINTE-BEUVE ON BÉRANGER 169
    LOWELL ON BÉRANGER 172
    GOETHE ON ROUSSEAU 173
    GRILLPARZER ON ROUSSEAU 175

CONTENTS

PAGE

SAINTE-BEUVE ON ROUSSEAU 178
LOWELL ON ROUSSEAU 182
GRILLPARZER ON VICTOR HUGO 186
SAINTE-BEUVE ON VICTOR HUGO 189
LOWELL ON VICTOR HUGO 191

GERMAN LITERATURE
GOETHE ON LESSING 194
GRILLPARZER ON LESSING 194
LOWELL ON LESSING 197
GOETHE ON SCHILLER 204
GRILLPARZER ON SCHILLER 206
GRILLPARZER ON GOETHE 207
GRILLPARZER ON GOETHE'S " ELECTIVE AFFINITIES " 208
GRILLPARZER APROPOS OF " ECKERMANN'S CONVERSA-
    TIONS WITH GOETHE " 210
GRILLPARZER ON GOETHE AND SCHILLER . . . 211
SAINTE-BEUVE ON GOETHE 212
LOWELL ON GOETHE 216
LOWELL ON CLASSIC AND MODERN FORMS IN GERMAN
    LITERATURE 220

ITALIAN LITERATURE
GOETHE ON DANTE 223
GRILLPARZER ON DANTE 224
SAINTE-BEUVE ON DANTE 226
LOWELL ON DANTE 228

SPANISH LITERATURE
GOETHE ON CALDERON 237
GRILLPARZER ON CALDERON 237
LOWELL ON CALDERON 241
GRILLPARZER ON LOPE DE VEGA 242
GRILLPARZER ON THE CONTRAST BETWEEN SPANISH
    AND GERMAN DRAMATISTS 244
GRILLPARZER ON CERVANTES 245
LOWELL ON CERVANTES 248

THE ANCIENTS
GOETHE ON EURIPIDES 256
GOETHE ON THE GREEK TRAGEDIANS 257

CONTENTS

	PAGE
GRILLPARZER ON EURIPIDES	259
GRILLPARZER ON THE GREEK CHORUS	265
LOWELL ON THE GREEKS	266
LOWELL'S CONTRAST BETWEEN ANCIENTS AND MODERNS	267
LOWELL ON THE GREEK AND THE MODERN DRAMA	272
WHAT IS A CLASSIC?	
GOETHE'S ANSWER	275
SAINTE-BEUVE'S ANSWER	277
LOWELL'S ANSWER	278
PHILOSOPHY AND RELIGION	
GOETHE ON LAVATER	281
GOETHE ON SPINOZA	282
GOETHE ON THE BIBLE	285
GRILLPARZER ON RELIGIOUS ANTAGONISMS	290
GRILLPARZER ON HEGEL	291
GOETHE ON LITERATURE AS INFLUENCED BY SURROUNDINGS	292
LESSONS FROM THE MASTERS	295

ILLUSTRATIONS

James Russell Lowell . . . . . . *Frontispiece*

FACING PAGE

Goethe on the Campagna 87

Franz Grillparzer 110

Charles-Augustin Sainte-Beuve 212

(From "Charles-Augustin Sainte-Beuve" by George Mc-
Lean Harper, published by J. B. Lippincott Company)

INTRODUCTION

"I am convinced," says Lessing, "that no nation on earth has a monopoly of intellect in any of its manifestations. I know very well that people talk of the profoundly serious Englishmen and the witty Frenchmen, but who has made this distinction? Surely not Nature, who impartially distributes all her gifts. There are just as many witty Englishmen as witty Frenchmen, and just as many profoundly serious Frenchmen as profoundly serious Englishmen." We have in these words an implied declaration of his belief, borne out by all his teachings, that intellect recognizes no distinctions of nationality, race, or religion.

Chauvinistic criticism of foreign achievement is merely proof of inability to criticise at all. Herder condemns the expression, "the races of mankind," as "ignoble words." And if the philosopher and scientist is thus admonished to divest himself of a prejudice which would segregate mankind along narrow and arbitrary lines, with how much greater force comes the warning to the literary critic, who is solely concerned with the beautiful in human thought and expression.

English literature has always been rich in writers of remarkable gifts, of wide knowledge and high ideals, but these have not all possessed that precious gift which leads the thinkers of one nation to regard those of another with genuine sympathy. Matthew Arnold deplored the absence of this feeling in Coleridge, who was unable to find high literary genius in the French; yet, in turn, Arnold himself was not always just towards Germans, and far from being in full sympathy with Americans. The French, perhaps, have had more reason than most other nations to complain that their literary ideals were misunderstood by foreigners. Gaston Deschamps has spoken with considerable force of German injustice towards France, but while defending the fair fame of his country, he has his fling at Germany as the deifier of pure force in literature. That nothing is gained for the cause of good taste and mutual good-will by mutual recriminations of this kind is very evident. Fortunately, every nation can furnish a few critics whose international standards are directly helpful in bringing about a better mutual understanding between civilised countries.

Among the eminent writers of present-day England, John Morley and James Bryce are international critics in the fullest sense of the word. Oliver Wendell Holmes, among our own great writers of the past, possessed in full measure active sympathy with other nations. Writing from Paris to his parents, at the age of twenty-five, he said: "One of the greatest pleasures of living abroad is to meet in such an easy, pleasant sort of a way people from all quarters of the world. Greek and Barbarian, Jew and Gentile, differ much less than one thinks." We recognise in the language of the young American student the spirit of the future cosmopolitan thinker—the spirit of an Epictetus and a Montaigne.

Unfortunately, the day has not yet passed when the interests of nations were supposed to be diametrically opposite to each other. In literature East and West are perhaps further apart than they were a hundred years ago, when Friedrich Schlegel wrote: "The dwellers in Asia and the people of Europe ought to be treated in popular works as members of one vast family, and their history will never be separated by any student anxious fully to comprehend the bearing of the whole; but the idea of Oriental genius in literature generally entertained in the present day is founded on that of a few Asiatic writers only, the Persians and Arabs in particular, and a few books of the Old Testament, in so far as we may be permitted to view the latter as poetry; but there are many other Asiatic nations to whom this ordinary

opinion is by no means applicable." Few, indeed,
are the great writers who have heard the call
of the Orient, few the critics who, by virtue of
their international interests, have attained international significance.

I have ventured to gather into these pages a
few specimens from the writings of four literary
critics of acknowledged power and importance—
writers whom the literatures of Germany, Austria, France and America cherish among their
greatest possessions, who were deeply imbued
with the national spirit and endowed with international sympathies, who surveyed mankind and
its past achievements with a philosophic gaze,
who studied and thought as long as they lived,
and looked for beauty in literature, finding expression for the perfect things which their search
revealed in beautiful words of their own. It has
seemed to me that by bringing into juxtaposition
certain passages from Goethe, Grillparzer, Sainte-
Beuve and Lowell, on subjects which engaged
their thought in common, I could best illustrate
their critical methods, which differed as widely
as did their personal and literary characteristics.
Needless to say, only the briefest outline of these
characteristics can be attempted within the compass of this volume. But even the most cursory

survey of the activity of the four critics with whom these pages are concerned discloses certain marked resemblances and differences.

Though there have been greater scholars in special fields who followed the critical calling, no other literary critics brought to their task more varied knowledge and a clearer perception of the dignity of literary achievement. The value of what they said was enforced by the excellence of what they did. All four were careful and keen-eyed observers; each of them taught and practised that, while in veneration for the literary traditions of the past, and in close study of the great models, are rooted the guiding principles of criticism, the literary man, above all, must live in the present and satisfy the demands of the hour. They had a clear eye for the realities of life and inculcated and practised good citizenship. All four rose to high public station, though Lowell alone was consistently active in the political developments of his country. It was their common lot to be accused of lack of patriotism, but each answered and refuted nobly the criticism of his political adversaries. Goethe, occupying the highest positions in the duchy of Saxe-Weimar, Grillparzer as member, in his old age, of the Austrian House of Peers, Sainte-Beuve as French Senator,

Lowell as American Minister in Spain and England—all bore their public dignities easily and worthily.

Goethe, Grillparzer, Sainte-Beuve, and Lowell alike had to contend against the physical depressions to which literary men are peculiarly prone, and which in the case of Grillparzer and Lowell were accentuated by inheritance; but they all conquered their weaknesses by sheer will-power and reliance on intellectual resources. They rose, like all lofty minds, into regions of serenity. Their idealism, as reflected in their critical standards, bears no trace of physical infirmity or mental indecision. Contradictions there are in their critical utterances, but we see in these merely varying aspects of the subject due to changing moods and the flight of time. Personal prejudice but rarely clouds their literary judgment.

While neither Grillparzer nor Lowell had the encyclopædic range of knowledge over which Goethe's vision swept, nor the familiarity with the natural sciences which the study of medicine had brought to Sainte-Beuve, they seized as eagerly as Goethe and Sainte-Beuve what served their purpose. We find Lowell early in his career devoting many hours each day to the study of German and Spanish, and he mastered the latter language perhaps even more completely than Grillparzer, though he did not draw the same inspiration from its poets.

Goethe, Grillparzer, Sainte-Beuve, and Lowell alike sought to the last the companionship of wise books, and their critical faculty remained undimmed in old age. Eleven days before his death Goethe writes to his friend Zelter a letter in the liveliest strain; his mind is occupied with "all sorts of examples from ancient history," with an archæological discovery of great personal interest to him, but whose intrinsic importance, he says, one ought to be careful not to overrate: he speaks of remains of fossil animals and plants that are accumulating around him: he finds that it has become the fashion for English, French, and Germans "to express themselves in an incomprehensible manner," and he longs for "the emphatic language of some Italian." And he praises Zelter for remaining "firm in the midst of what is fleeting." "As for myself," he says, "living chiefly in the past, less in the future, and at present thinking of what is very remote, you will bear in mind that I am quite content."

Sainte-Beuve, for years in the agonies of a cruel and, as he realized, hopeless malady, kept on writing with stoic determination for the *Temps*, almost to the last hour. Grillparzer's closing eyes rested on a volume of the Greek tragedian who,

above all others, had been his solace in life. Lowell abandoned his reading only with life itself.
During his last illness, "his books," in the words
of his biographer, Horace E. Scudder, "were close
at hand and his constant friends. He re-read
Boswell's *Johnson* for the fourth time, and he
read the recently published full diary of Walter
Scott. He took up novel reading, rather a new
taste, and amused himself with contemporaneous
society in England as depicted by Norris. . . .
Death found him cheerful."

Such was the consistent attitude toward life and
literature of these eminently representative men
of letters. Theirs was—with all the differences
of temperament and personal characteristics—a
self-contained repose, as free from flippant self-
sufficiency as it was from the shallow optimism
which sees in the things of this world the best of
all possible things. Though Lowell betrayed the
Puritan strain in his blood and professed a certain allegiance to inherited faith, and though
Sainte-Beuve sometimes toyed with Catholicism,
they ranged themselves with Goethe and Grillparzer on the side of intellectual independence
concerning all the religious movements that have
left their impress on literature and swayed thinking men. All four, no matter what their subject,
spoke from the depth of conviction. We feel at

all times the sheer intellectual force of their utterances, and we yield to the charm of their diction. Of each of them, at his best, is true what Emerson said of Montaigne: "Cut his words, and they bleed."

It is needless to say that what is offered in this volume is neither biography nor analysis. The author, however, entertains the hope that his comparison of the four critics, and their own opinions on the subjects chosen for illustration, may here and there interest students of literature. The careful reader will not mistake the necessarily brief extracts for their authors' final judgments. Sainte-Beuve may, in a petulant moment, speak of Goethe as "that Talleyrand in his art," but no one who knows Sainte-Beuve can be in doubt as to the depth of his admiration for Goethe. Grillparzer occasionally chafes under Goethe's supremacy, just as he rebels against the "tyranny" of Shakespeare, but his protest is in itself the warmest tribute to their master intellects. Goethe, Grillparzer and Lowell permitted themselves to criticise Lessing, precisely because they recognised in him the most fearless of critics.

The reader, it is hoped, will not quarrel with the latitude which the author has allowed himself in the choice of his selections and in giving, now to one writer, now to another, the principal share in the discussion of any one subject. Collectively, he believes, these extracts will convey, as far as extracts can, an adequate impression of the masterfulness of all the four critics. At best, however, they are no more than hints of what is in store for those who will abandon themselves to the full enjoyment of writers who so amply repay close study. The brief specimens culled from their pages cannot give an adequate idea of the characteristic qualities of each, but they may arouse sufficient interest in the reader to send him back to the sources themselves—to Goethe's all-embracing wisdom and majestic objectivity, to Grillparzer's incisive originality, to Sainte-Beuve's almost unvarying perfection of form and easy mastery of detail, and to Lowell's moral earnestness and flashing wit.

A word as to the apparently disproportionate space given to the American critic may not be out of place. Lowell, aside from England, is as little known to Europeans as was Grillparzer for so many years to Americans. It is the hope of the author that by linking Lowell's name with the names of Goethe, Grillparzer, and Sainte-Beuve he may contribute something, in however modest a degree, towards awakening, on the other side of the ocean, interest in a writer whose critical and scholarly achievements, no less than his personality, made him so worthy a representative of American literature.

GOETHE'S UNIVERSAL INTERESTS

SAINTE-BEUVE speaks of Goethe as the greatest of all critics. He certainly stands alone in the comprehensiveness of his intellectual sympathies and the vastness of his knowledge, in the manifestations of a powerful, creative genius finding critical utterance. All the phases of Goethe's activity have been amply discussed in that vast Goethe literature to which all nations have contributed, but something, it would seem, is still to be said of his unique importance as an international critic.

Wisdom such as Goethe possessed is not learned from books; he looked upon life and men, upon literature, science, and art with equal interest and equal detachment. The world can show no other example of so much creative power joined to so much critical acumen. His poetic productions, as he so often pointed out, were born of the impulse of the moment, his critical wisdom was the result of life-long self-restraint. His attitude was always judicial, though at times there was in his judgments a certain lack of finality, as if he felt the need of still wider information. His intellectual curiosity was endless, though kept within

1

bounds by his natural reposefulness. He allowed
nothing to claim his attention exclusively. It was
his aim to rise above the merely transitory and
fasten upon the permanent. His sympathies were
too general to be expended upon any one phase of
individual effort. Nor does this imply, as has
sometimes been charged, a certain aristocratic
aloofness in Goethe's character. "It was natural
for me," he says in his autobiography, "to enter
into the conditions of other men, to sympathise
with every phase of man's existence and to find
pleasure in sharing it." We feel this universal
sympathy in Goethe's critical attitude toward not-
able literary efforts of whatever kind. He approaches the most diverse subjects with equal interest and equal desire to learn the truth. He
discusses, as a young man, the poems of an obscure
Polish Jew quite as philosophically as a scientific
treatise on the clouds, or Shakespeare's *Cymbeline*.
No other critic has given to the world such ripe
and varied results of self-culture. His literary susceptibilities sprang from the ever deepening conviction that all mankind is related to the truly educated man. He adopted and expanded the saying
of Epictetus: "Never, in reply to the question
to what country you belong, say that you are an
Athenian or a Corinthian, but say that you are a
citizen of the world."

In this noble cosmopolitanism lay Goethe's supreme importance as literary critic. The love of one's own country is natural to everybody and need not be inculcated, but our interest in other nations can be strengthened and kept alive only by active sympathy and deliberate effort. "The poet," said Goethe to Eckermann, "loves his native land as a man and citizen, but the fatherland of his poetic powers and his poetic activity is the good and noble and beautiful, and that is not limited to any particular province or any particular country.* He seizes it and makes use of it wherever he finds it. He may be likened to the eagle who soars over the land with wide gaze, and is indifferent as to whether the hare upon which he suddenly descends is running on Prussian or Saxon soil. What, in reality, does it mean to love one's own country and be patriotic? If a poet has all his life endeavoured to overcome harmful prejudices and narrow views, to enlighten his countrymen, improve their tastes, and ennoble their feelings and thoughts, could he have been better employed, and rendered a more patriotic service?"

* Lowell expresses the same thought in the lines:
   "Where is the true man's fatherland?
   Is it where he by chance is born?
   Doth not the yearning spirit scorn
   In such scant borders to be spanned?"

Amid the endless variety of subjects to which
Goethe's critical sagacity was applied throughout
life, his vision ever remained clear. He discerned
every object that came within his ken, and analysed carefully whatever appealed to him. No
other critic of modern times inspires us with the
same confidence in his competence to speak of matters outside of the chosen field in which he is the
recognised master; no one had the same background of ripe experience, the same fund of wisdom on which he could endlessly draw. No other
critic has so constantly pointed out, by his own example, the interdependence of literature, art and
science. Just as, in conversation with his friends,
he passed rapidly from topic to topic, culling from
the many fields over which his mind continually
ranged, so in his contact with the affairs of life he
turned from occupation to occupation, "without
haste, without rest." Nothing can be more instructive in this respect than to show how many
activities Goethe could crowd into a single year,
although, as applied to him, the word "crowded"
seems ill-chosen, to such a degree was constant
and varied activity a necessity of his nature. Let
us take, at random, his notes for the year 1817, in
the *Annalen*.

"For more than one reason," he writes, "I
had during this year to make a prolonged stay in

Jena, and foreseeing this, I sent there some of my manuscripts, drawings, apparatus and collections. But first of all, I inspected the various institutions, and finding much that seemed important in its bearing on the formation and transformation of plants, I established a separate botanical museum.''

He also rearranged, during this year, the university library, which was in a state of neglect and confusion, as well as the veterinary school. Among the other subjects to which he devoted attention at the same period were the following: The anatomy of caterpillars and butterflies, the influence of Kant on his own philosophical studies, geology, mineralogy and kindred sciences, the precious stones of Brazil, the polarisation of light and chromatics. Everything assumed additional importance in his hands through his tendency to connect the remote with the present. Thus he says, in the entry referred to:

''I owed much enlightenment in geology and geography to Sorriot's map of the mountains of Europe; through it, for example, the land and the soil of Spain, so troublesome to a commanding general and so favourable to guerilla warfare, became at once clear to me. I drew the principal water-sheds on my own map of Spain, and every campaign, every route, all the regular and irregu-

lar army movements became plain and intelligible.'' Plastic art, as usual, claimed much of his
attention. His desire to see the Elgin marbles at
that time was so great that ''one fine, sunny
morning, starting to drive from my house without any particular purpose, I suddenly turned,
overcome by my desire, towards Rudolstadt,
where I refreshed myself by gazing long on the
truly wonderful heads of Monte Cavallo.'' He
studied minutely Bossi's work on Leonardo da
Vinci's ''Last Supper'' as well as pen drawings, engravings and lithographs, statuary and
archæological remains, observed the scattering
of the seed of the barberry flower, ''casually
made it my business to purge an old edition of
Thomas Campanella's *De sensu rerum* from
printer's errors''; turned with pleasure ''after
dwelling long on clouds and their forms'' to a
translation of the Hindu *Megha-Duta,* grew ''into
the habit of reading Byron,'' found in John
Hunter's *Life* ''a most important monument of a
splendid mind which, without school learning, developed nobly and powerfully,'' and contrasted
with it the *Life of Franklin,* which, ''while of the
same general character,'' was ''as wide apart
from it as the heavens.'' From Elphinstone's
Cabul and Raffle's *History of Java* he ''profited
immensely.'' Among other books that influenced

him during the year were Hermann's *De Myth-
ologia Græcorum antiquissima* and Raynouard's
Recherches sur l'ancienneté de la langue romane.

Such many-sidedness implied necessarily the
ability to keep at a distance subjects that had
ceased to interest him. Thus he rarely recurred
to Rousseau after he reached maturity, although
he had been greatly influenced by him in his youth.
But what had entered deeply into his intellectual
life became his permanent possession. He never
ceased to draw inspiration from the ancients,
never abated his admiration for Shakespeare, or
Molière, or Spinoza.

Much has been said of Goethe's interest in
world-literature. In its essence, his effort to
foster an international appreciation of the master
works of all time was a protest against national
one-sidedness. But such an appreciation was con-
ditioned on critical capacity to distinguish between the commonplace good and the commanding best. There is narrowness in too wide a tolerance of mediocrity. Such narrowness was impossible to Goethe, not only, as Professor J. R.
Seeley has remarked, because his mind was large,
but because he realised that the German public in
their good-natured tolerance had made themselves
familiar with far too great a variety of ideas.
"In our estimate of foreign writers," Goethe

said, "we must not fasten upon national characteristics and imagine that they are to serve as our
model. We must not single out the Chinese, or
the Servian, or Calderon, or the Nibelungenlied;
but if we look for a model of what is really excellent we must return again and again to the ancient Greeks, in whose works man in all his beauty
appears to us. All the rest is only of a historic
interest, and we may use what good there is in it
as far as it serves our purpose." Goethe disliked
provincialism in literature, just as he deprecated
sectarianism in religion and chauvinism in politics. International hatred was utterly inconceivable to him. There were certain patriots who reproached him with not having taken up arms during the War of Liberation, or at least with not
having encouraged it as a poet.

"Let us not speak of this," said Goethe on this
subject to Eckermann; "we live in a foolish
world, which does not know what it wants; we
must allow it to have its say. How could I take
up arms without being impelled thereto by hatred?
And how could I hate at my age? Had those
events happened when I was twenty years of age,
I should surely not have been the last to take up
arms, but they took place when I was past sixty.
Besides, we cannot all serve our country in the
same way. Each of us must do the best God has

enabled him to do. I have toiled hard enough for half a century. I may say that in those matters which nature has fitted me to do as my daily task, I have allowed myself no rest or relaxation by day or night; I have always toiled, studied, and aimed at progress as far and as well as I could. If each of us can say the same thing of himself, it will be well with all of us. . . .

"To write military songs, sitting in my room— that would indeed have suited my nature! Camping in the open air, by night, with the horses of the enemy's outposts neighing near me, that would have been more to my liking. But this was not my affair, nor the object of my life. That was the business of Theodor Körner; his martial songs suited his nature perfectly. But war is foreign to me, and I am without military ambition; martial songs would therefore have been merely a mask, which would have ill fitted me.

"I have never affected anything in my poetry. I have never thought and expressed anything that did not live within me and inspire me irresistibly. I have never written love songs except when I loved; how then could I have written songs of hatred without hating? And between ourselves, I never hated the French, although I thanked God when we were rid of them. How could I, to whom the question of culture and barbarism alone is all-important, hate a nation which is among the most cultured of the world, and to which I owe so great a part of my own culture? National hatred is indeed a peculiar thing. It is always found most pronounced and violent where civilisation is lowest; but there is a stage of culture where it vanishes altogether, where one stands, so to say, above all nations, and feels the happiness and the sorrows of a neighbouring people as much as if they were a part of one's own. This degree of culture was in accord with my nature, and I had become confirmed in these views before I reached my sixtieth year.''

The creation of a world-literature was, in Goethe's eyes, the natural result of an intelligent and humane interest in other nations than one's own. ''It is very gratifying,'' he said, ''that the close relations existing between French, English and Germans make it possible for these nations to correct each other. We, perhaps, can appreciate Shakespeare and Byron better than the English.''

Numerous passages scattered throughout Goethe's writings testify to his appreciation of the peculiar importance of English literature. He often laid stress on the value of becoming familiar with the English language and thus with the character of the British nation. He wrote to Countess O'Donell, July 24, 1813: ''I congratulate you sincerely on your interest in the English language. Its literature offers the vastest treasures, and it is scarcely possible to appreciate all its wealth on first approaching it."

In one of his minor scientific papers (''Materialien zur Geschichte der Farbenlehre'') he remarks, with reference to Newton's personality: "What chiefly characterises the English, and cannot be too highly praised, is that they make it possible for so many sound and straightforward individuals to develop themselves, each in his own way, while at the same time serving the public and the commonwealth. This is an advantage which perhaps no other nation possesses, at least not to the same extent." Elsewhere, in these notes on scientific subjects, he says: "The English possess, perhaps above most nations, the ability to impress themselves upon foreigners. Their personal repose, precision, industry, firmness of opinion and complacency, form an almost unapproachable model of what everybody would wish to attain."

Goethe's critical activity, strictly speaking, extended over sixty years. He began to write for the *Frankfurter Gelehrte Anzeigen* in 1772, when twenty-three years of age, and his earliest contributions showed that seriousness and maturity which characterised all his critical work. He wrote on Sulzer's Theory of the Fine Arts, on

Homer and Shakespeare, on the Truths of Revelation, on Paradise and Eternity, on Lavater's Ser-
mons, on a work about Turkish Laws, on a treatise
concerning the Characteristics of the Principal
European Nations, on a scientific System of Nature, etc. Of greater importance were his subsequent contributions, on a vast range of literary,
scientific, linguistic, and æsthetic subjects, which
appeared in Wieland's *Merkur,* in the *Propyläen,*
in *Kunst und Alterthum,* and the *Jenaische Allgemeine Literaturzeitung.* Painting, sculpture,
architecture, and the drama at all times claimed
his critical attention. In a larger sense his entire
life was devoted to the exposition of his views on
these subjects, and his critical activity was only
varied, but not interrupted, by his creative work.
His *Autobiography (Dichtung und Wahrheit)* and
Wilhelm Meister contain literary and philosophical criticism of the highest value, and we must go
not only to *Faust,* but also to the *Elective Affinities,* and even to *Tasso* and *Iphigenia,* if we would
have full insight into Goethe's philosophical and
critical methods. His *Annalen,* and his correspondence with Schiller, with the Humboldts,
with Zelter, and with other friends, are inexhaustible critical repositories, but even these are
surpassed in value by his talks with Eckermann.
In Eckermann's *Conversations with Goethe* the

great thinker stands before us in all the benignant
wisdom of his last decade.   Nowhere else does he
so fully impress us with the comprehensiveness of
his judgment on literature and life.

It is characteristic of Goethe's attitude towards
life and literature that even in his earliest book
notices philosophical reflection predominates over
critical analysis.   He was never a professional
critic in the usual sense of the word.   Books of
doubtful value he scarcely ever read or alluded to,
either in writing or in conversation; but he recurred again and again to the excellent, expatiat-
ing upon previously uttered thoughts that seemed
to him to require amplification, and comparing the
great writers and artists of one nation with those
of another.   It will be seen, in the extracts given
elsewhere, how difficult it is in the case of Goethe
to select passages illustrative of any one subject,
so closely are reflections upon many others inter-
woven with the main text.   The French are contrasted with the ancients, Béranger suggests Horace or Hafiz; from Voltaire and priestcraft we
pass to the fossiliferous formation of some German mountain.   Everywhere we see the hand of
wisdom pointing to some new outlook upon the
world.   Let us quote, from his hitherto untrans-
lated earliest contributions to the *Frankfurter
Gelehrte Anzeigen,* the review of Robert Wood's

Essay on the Original Genius of Homer. Goethe was speaking of a German version of the English work.

"No other European nation," he said, "possesses the enthusiasm of the British for the remains of antiquity, an enthusiasm which spares neither money nor trouble in restoring them, if possible, in all their former glory. The recent work of the French merchant Guys, who contrasted the ancient and modern Greeks, was mere child's-play compared with the merits of what Wood has done concerning Homer. If we would enter into the genius of the most venerable of all poets, we must not expect help from either Aristotle or Bossu. Neither shall we find in Wood the empty formulas which Blair employed in elucidating Ossian, or those used by a certain female commentator in her Shakespeare apology. If we would fully appreciate the originality of Homer, we must start with the conviction that he owed to himself and to Mother Nature all he was; and this is clearly impossible without the minutest knowledge of his time and of the locality where he sang his songs. Our knowledge of the age must be derived, since there are no monuments of it extant, from his own language, and from the locality, which has become familiar only through travel. Both these points have hitherto been totally neglected by a great number of his commentators. Wood studied his Homer with philosophical eyes and made more than one journey to the regions made famous by the Iliad and Odyssey, whose physical status has on the whole remained unchanged. He was one of the company of travellers who have erected an imperishable monument to themselves out of the ruins of Baalbek and Palmyra. He devoted to the study of Homer •the greater part of a life which unfortunately has now ended. What we see in his book are but fragments of a general commentary upon the father of poetry which he intended to write, and which would have been unique of its kind. The lack of careful arrangement, the existence of many gaps and the frequent references to a more elaborate future work give to this treatise the appearance of incompleteness. We have nevertheless in it most precious fragments, which can only make us regret more deeply the loss of the principal work, unless indeed the heir of the author, Mr. Bryant, should have been fortunate enough to find it among his posthumous papers. With the clearest eye he penetrates the fog that surrounds the distant culture of the Homeric age and teaches us to look at the history of mankind from a philosophical point of view. Let us take, as an example, his remarks on navigation, as practised in

that age, and on the formation of the Greek language. Ignorance concerning these matters has
produced innumerable worthless judgments, unfortunately repeated in certain comments upon
the Iliad recently published in Vienna. Wood's
knowledge of the locality has enabled him, for instance, to throw a new light on the Homeric ma-
chines, to explain the faults of Pope's chart, to decide the famous dispute as to the distance of the
Isle of Pharus from the mainland, etc.

"The genius of Virgil has also in several passages been admirably described. Even when the active mind of the author loses itself in such bold
conjectures as those upon Homer's native land, or
upon the chronology of the Homeric age, we must
admire the thinker, although we may not wholly
agree with him. Taken from its context, what he
says seems to imply that the ancients did not study
their Homer with proper attention to locality, nor
in the proper spirit. And if we read the entire
book itself, we shall be forced to admit that the
critical opinions concerning Homer which have
come down to us from antiquity are far below the
views which Wood opens up to us. For the honor
of the ancients, however, let us assume that their
most valuable researches concerning Homer were
lost in the course of the ages."

Sixty years later, in 1832—the year of his death

—Goethe still recurred to the subject of the heroic age of Greece, in an elaborate notice of Spontini's opera, *The Women of Athens.*

Of great intrinsic importance are Goethe's reflections called forth by the activity of the French periodical, *Le Globe,* to which, in the last years of his life, before it became an organ of Saint-Simonism, he paid much attention. The writers in the *Globe,* among whom was Sainte-Beuve, appeared to him to have grasped clearly the meaning of his world-literature, and the admiration bestowed by able commentators in that periodical on his own dramatic works filled him with genuine pleasure. In addition to the *Globe* he read with interest several of the most important British reviews, whose contributions likewise testified to the spread of international relations in literature. He anticipated, however, the objections to an indiscriminate and artificial identification of literary interests among the nations of the world, and laid the greatest stress on the need of serious individual effort and the cultivation of one's native talent.

"Vast as the world is," he wrote, "it is but an enlarged fatherland, and, if we look at the matter closely, it cannot give us more than our native soil can furnish. What pleases the multitude is sure to gain unbounded popularity and, as we see, spreads to the furthest countries and to every clime; but what is serious and important is less certain of such a result. Nevertheless, those who devote themselves to higher ideals and to what is productive in the best sense will henceforth come into more rapid and closer contact. There are in every part of the world men interested in what has been long established and must serve as a base for the true progress of humanity. But their ways are not the ways of the average man, nor can their pace be followed; those who live for the enjoyment of life demand a more rapid rate of progress, and hence refuse to be led and to aid in the cause which they ought to serve. The serious-minded, therefore, must form a quiet and self-contained community; it were useless to oppose the broad current of the hour, but it is well to maintain courageously one's firm attitude until the flood has passed. The principal consolation and encouragement that such men will find is that what is true is also useful. . . . Every nation has peculiarities which distinguish it from other nations, and it is these characteristics which mutually attract and repel. An inner peculiarity is in its outward manifestation often very obnoxious to another nation, or if not so, appears at least ridiculous. For these reasons we always appreciate every nation less fully than it deserves. The inner traits are neither known nor recognised, not only by strangers, but by the very nation itself. The real nature, with nations as with individuals, is beneath the surface, and we are astonished at its sudden manifestation.''

Goethe often spoke in a similar strain about the importance of looking at life and literature from a wider point of view than the purely national one; thus he said, in a review of Serb folk-songs: ''The purely human repeats itself among all nations, but it inspires no real interest when it appears in a foreign garb or under a foreign sky; what is particularly characteristic of every nation produces only a strange and often a disagreeable impression, like everything peculiar the proper significance of which we have not grasped, and which we have therefore not yet learned to understand.''

It is instructive to recall with what minute interest Goethe followed the course of the *Edinburgh Review* and the *Foreign Quarterly Review,* in whose leading articles he must have been glad to discern a reflection of his own critical spirit. He wrote, in 1828:

''These periodicals, as they gradually gain a larger public, will contribute most effectually to that hoped-for universal world-literature; but we repeat that there can be no idea of a general

agreement of thought among nations; all we can
expect is that they may learn to see each other in
the proper light, to understand and tolerate each
other even if there can be no mutual affection
among them.   There exist now several institutions whose purpose it is to make the British Isles
acquainted with other nations, and as there is sub-
stantial agreement in these efforts, we foreigners
learn in this way what is thought about us in
England and how we are being judged.   On the
whole, we gladly admit that these agencies pro-
ceed seriously and studiously, that the writers are
well informed and thoroughly sympathetic.   The
results for us will be that we shall be led to take
up again and consider anew our own literature,
which in some respects, though still recent, we
had already begun to lay aside.   It is quite remarkable to notice, how, beginning with some
prominent author, these reviewers take occasion
to survey the entire field in which he labored;
thus, starting with the works of Wilhelm Hoff-
mann they speak of the admissibility of the supernatural in works of fiction. . . . In discussing
Victor Cousin's *Philosophical Fragments,* German philosophy in general comes in for unfavour-
able comment, and the writer finally identifies
himself with Jacobi's doctrine of the emotions.
The Letters of a German Traveller caused the re-

viewer to range himself on the side of those who would wish to see Germany as a great unit, with a great capital as its center.''

Goethe often held up the directness of the English style as a model to his countrymen. He said to Eckermann:

''On the whole, philosophical speculations are injurious to the Germans, as they infuse into their literary style something vague, intangible and obscure. The stronger their adherence to certain philosophic schools, the worse they write. Those Germans, however, who, as business-men and men of the world, look only to the practical side of things, write best. Schiller's style is most brilliant and impressive when he ceases to philosophise, as I see in his letters, which I am just now looking over, and which are of the highest importance. There are also gifted German women who write admirably, and, indeed, they are in this respect superior to some of our famous male authors.

''The English, as a rule, write uniformly well, being born orators and men of practical sense, busy with realities. The French, in their style, are true to their general character. Their nature is social, and they never forget what is due to the public whom they address. They endeavour to be clear, so as to convince the reader, and agreeable, so as to please him.

"All in all, the style of an author is the true image of his mind. He who would write clearly, ought first to think clearly, and whoever would have a grand style must first have a grand character."

Genius, in Goethe's conception of the term, implied character. He thus expresses himself to Eckermann as to the harm done by writers who lacked, in their very nature, the elements of real greatness: "Want of character, in individual investigators and writers is the source of all the evils in our recent literature. In criticism especially, this defect produces great harm." He sighed for another Lessing, for one of his character and firmness. The greatest ability, if not employed in the pursuit of high aims, merely repelled him. Two months before his death, in speaking to Eckermann about Victor Hugo's great productivity, he remarked: "Can a writer help deteriorating and ruining even a very great talent, if he has the hardihood to write in a single year two tragedies and a novel, and if, moreover, he seems to write only in order to amass a great deal of money? I by no means blame him for trying to become rich, nor for seeking the fame of the day, but if he wishes to be remembered by posterity he must begin to write less and to work more."

In his teachings as in his practice, Goethe enforced the need of keeping at a distance the vulgar which threatens to enthrall us all. "Men are so prone," says Wilhelm Meister, "to give themselves up to the commonplace and vulgar, the mind and the feelings so easily become callous to the beautiful and the perfect, that one ought to try in every way possible to retain a taste for higher things. Such enjoyments no one can wholly do without. Our lack of familiarity with what is really excellent is the explanation why so many take pleasure in what is silly and insipid, merely because it is new. We ought to form the habit of listening every day to some pretty song, reading a fine poem, looking at a beautiful picture and, if possible, talking a few sensible words."

GRILLPARZER'S ORIGINALITY AS CRITIC

GRILLPARZER's critical writings are virtually unknown to English readers. Even in Germany his fame as a dramatist has completely overshadowed every other phase of his intellectual activity. Possibly the day may come when literary historians will recognise in him a great critic, just as they are gradually awakening to the fact that world literature possesses in him one of its greatest dramatic writers. His popularity at the present day certainly rivals that of any other German classic. We learn from the introduction to the definitive edition of his collected works, which the city of Vienna honours itself in publishing, that the Cottas, who secured the copyright of Grillparzer's work after his death, printed within thirty years 1,500,000 volumes in the various editions of his works. Books about him have been written in English, French, Italian, and Swedish, and in the words of one of his most competent biographers, Professor August Sauer—the editor of the Vienna edition—Grillparzer's fame "as one of the greatest dramatic poets of all times and all nations is firmly established." Yet George

24

Saintsbury and Edward Dowden were the first English literary authorities who grasped the significance of Grillparzer's critical utterances. In his essay, "Is Shakespeare Self-Revealed?" Dowden says:

"Next in rank to Goethe and Schiller among the classical dramatists who have written in the German language stands Grillparzer. He was a close student of Shakespeare and of Lope de Vega. His plays, ideal like the *Hero and Leander* and the *Medea*, or historical like *King Ottokar* and *The True Servant*, are, as are Shakespeare's plays, of an objective kind, although, it may be noticed in passing, one pretty incident from a love-passage of his own is transported bodily into the *Hero and Leander*, and the heroine of that play and the formidable heroine of the *Medea* were studied from persons whom he loved. It is of some interest to compare the view of an eminent dramatist concerning a craftsman in his own trade with the view of an eminent critic like Dr. Sidney Lee. Grillparzer censures Schiller for 'speaking too often himself without allowing his characters to speak.' He does not find Shakespeare guilty of this offence: but he does not suppose that Shakespeare evoked his world out of nothing or out of mere observation of men and books." Professor Dowden quotes Grillparzer's ideas as to Shakespeare's method of finding his subjects (which will be found in another part of this book) and he adds that Coleridge's remarks on the subject nearly coincide with Grillparzer's. Saintsbury remarks, in his *History of Criticism:* "I am told by persons who know more about the matter than I do, that Grillparzer was a remarkable playwright; I am sure that he is a remarkable critic."

Grillparzer was all his life a lover of good books of many nations. He studied Greek and Spanish dramatic literature, in particular, more constantly than did Goethe, Sainte-Beuve, or Lowell. For the portrayal of his characters and the development of his plots, he went to no source but his imagination: for his literary background he turned to volume after volume of recondite lore. And with all his ease in composition,—after the slow brooding time was over—only the constant exercise of severe self-criticism gave him that unerring felicity of phrase, that intimate adaptation of word to mood and action which marks the great literary artist.

As I have said elsewhere * : "Jotted down mostly on the spur of the moment, with no thought of publication, and covering, as they do, practically the entire period of his intellectual activity,

* *Franz Grillparzer and the Austrian Drama.*

his critical remarks are all the more interesting from their momentary point of view and not infrequent contradictions—the result of riper judgment and an invariable desire to be just. His lifelong study of the Greek dramatists is evidenced by a weighty paper on the significance of the chorus in the ancient tragedy, and particularly by numerous passages on Euripides, his favourite author among the ancients. An entire volume of the Cotta edition of Grillparzer's works is given up to his contributions to the study of the Spanish theatre, covering hundreds of plays. Of the masterpieces of the Spanish dramatists Grillparzer might often have said, in his moments of despondency, what Lowell wrote after the death of his second wife: 'I have at last found something I can read — Calderon.' Grillparzer studied Calderon, and even more Lope de Vega, with loving minuteness. To no other writer did he turn more frequently for inspiration than to the latter.''

While it may be said that Grillparzer was a critic primarily for his own creative purposes, his subjective attitude merely heightens the clearness and precision of his utterances, which serve all the purposes of the most exacting objective criticism. Neither Goethe, nor Sainte-Beuve, nor Lowell, possessed the gift of self-criticism to the same degree as Grillparzer. It may be doubted whether the verbal blemishes—his Austriacisms and apparent occasional lapses in grammatical construction—are not the result of direct intention, rather than of accidental carelessness; what is certain is that the consistency and individuality of his characters bear the imprint of that critical habit which he turned against himself as remorselessly as he did against others. It is a curious and most instructive fact that every one of Grillparzer's great dramas has been pronounced his masterpiece by some competent critic —a singular phenomenon in literary criticism which, if it does not demonstrate the caprice of critics, proves that every one of these plays possesses merits of the very highest order. It may be doubted whether as much can be said of the total output of any other great dramatist of modern times. Grillparzer analysed his own works sometimes morbidly, but, as a rule, dispassionately and in a spirit of philosophical and modest resignation. What he says, in his fragmentary autobiography, concerning the right of the general public to pronounce judgment on the dramatic worth of a play is as sane criticism as has ever been uttered on the subject. Referring to his *Medea* trilogy, he remarked:

"I have always attached great value to the

judgment of the public. As regards the conception of his play the dramatic poet must consult his own judgment, but as to whether in its execution he has depicted human nature as we find it in life, the public alone, as representing human nature, can tell him. The public is no judge, but a jury; it issues its verdict in the shape of approval or disapproval. Its right to judge is based not on knowledge of the law, but on spontaneous and natural feeling. Of this naturalness, which in northern Germany has been pushed into the background by pseudo-culture and blind imitation, there still exists in Austria a considerable remnant, combined with a susceptibility which, by proper guidance on the part of the poet, can be heightened to an incredible degree. The pleasure of such a public may not prove much, for it wishes, above all, to be amused, but its disapproval is in the highest degree instructive. In this case all it pronounced was a *succes d'estime.*"

His autobiography closed with this reference to his superb drama, *Des Meeres und der Liebe Wellen:*

"I had found a new dramatic subject, or rather an old one, which I took up again: *Hero and Leander.* A beautiful woman tempted me to represent her outward form, even if not her real being, as she passes through the vicissitudes of fortune. The somewhat affected title, *Des Meeres und der Liebe Wellen* (The Waves of the Sea and of Love), was to point at the outset to the romantic, or rather purely human, treatment of the ancient legend. My interest centred in the principal character, and therefore I crowded the other persons—nay, toward the end, the development of the story itself—further into the background than was really just. And yet it was these last acts that I wrote with the deepest sentiment, the outcome of my interest in the heroine. That the fourth act bored the spectators to some extent lay partly in my intention, . . . but there are also other things in the play that ought to have been different." Two weeks after the first performance of *Des Meeres und der Liebe Wellen* he penned the following criticism of the play:

"On the fifth of this month (April, 1831) *Hero und Leander* was performed. No success. The first three acts were vociferously applauded, but the last two were passed over in inattentive silence. It is sad indeed that the voice of the public coincides so fully with my own doubts. The fifth act is unfortunately only too effective, too theatrical (for which reason I always wanted to change it); it evidently suffered from the ineffectiveness of the fourth act, for it is impossible to produce an effect upon a public that has lost its interest. Curious indeed! I wrote just this fourth act with the deepest feeling; nowhere did I enter so closely into the situation, and I originally considered it particularly good; but when I rewrote the play, a year later, I could not any more find the key to it. There is evidently too little development in the whole of the play; it is fragmentary and the result rather of general enthusiasm than of particular interest in the subject itself—in other words, it is more of a sketch than of a picture. I had set myself a tremendous task. Had I succeeded, the result would have been a great gain for poetry. But I did not succeed, and yet, and yet! If I can succeed in keeping myself, by a few successful plays, within the ranks of the poets who are to last, there may come a time when the world will recognise the value of this fourth act, even though I only half attained what I aimed at.''

While conceding to the public the rôle of a jury, as far as the theatrical effectiveness of a play is concerned, he was, as we have seen, far from granting it the rights of a judge in purely literary matters. Moreover, much as he appreciated in theory, and illustrated in practice, spontaneity of sentiment and naturalness of expression (''Die Natürlichkeit der Empfindung'') he did not believe in "natural poets," and distrusted the ability of the people, as such, to produce a literary work of genius. He deprecated the glorification of folk-lore by literary historians and sought in every genuine poetic work, whether epic or lyric, for the individual author. The anonymous multitude never created anything great, he said, and added:

"Since Hegel threw doubt on the validity of individual talent and every wooden pedant found it convenient to deny the prerogative of intellectual endowment, the theory of poetry without poets was established. Epics were supposed to have been the outcome of simple folk-songs, which some one from the rabble had made and some Middle-High German pedant had put together at haphazard. In this way the entire nation was elevated to the rank of poets, and according to this theory of folk-poesy, there is no reason why every writer of poetic doggerel of our own day should not consider himself as laying the foundations for future Iliads and Odysseys."

Grillparzer recognised in the Nibelungenlied a mysterious work of great power and wonderful poetic charm, but to believe, he said, "that such a poem could have come out of the mouth of the common people is to assume the impossible."

Contrary to Goethe, who admired poetic perfection in literature regardless of the genre, and ranked Béranger as highly as he did Byron or Molière, Grillparzer assumed a certain gradation of values in literary form and .expression. To epigrams and satires he assigned the lowest rank, to the drama the highest. The distinction is significant. Grillparzer disclaimed for himself a place by the side of the greatest dramatic poets, and he set little store by the multitude of epigrammatic flings (admirable satires of their kind) in which, throughout his life, he attacked bureaucratic stupidity or retaliated against political and literary persecution. Like his critical utterances, these epigrams slumbered in the recesses of his writing-desk.

Like Goethe, Grillparzer could appreciate the critical standards of many nations, as embodied in works of great literary excellence, and puritanism in literary matters was as foreign to him as to Goethe. But he had a sovereign contempt, exemplified in his own literary practices, for offences against established æsthetic standards. He wrote of Swift:

"Have the publishers of Swift's works done well in including therein those obscene riddles the composing of which gave the Dean of St. Patrick, then nearly sixty years of age, so much pleasure? I believe they have. For in spite of the inexpressible pain these riddles have given me, they embody a great lesson. That is to say, they show to what even the highest intellectual gifts finally lead if unaccompanied by genuine warmth of heart. But my disappointment was none the less real, for I was on the point of learning to admire Swift, in spite of all his faults." *

Much as he loved the ancients, Grillparzer was far from being their imitator. Like Goethe, he believed that the poet must in his works reflect his inner life. When reproached with having made his Sappho express un-Greek sentiments, he merely remarked that he had written his play for Germans and not for Athenians. We shall else-where see his definition of the difference between the life of the Athenians and our own.

One quality, above all others, Grillparzer de-manded of every poet, no matter how great and in-dividual his gifts,—concentration of all his powers. Just as Goethe admonished the poets to "command poesy," so Grillparzer showed by his own example that only he can be successful in literature who is master of himself and of his sur-roundings as well as of his moods. He had no patience with those critical theories which see in the works of a genius the results of his time and the conditions of his milieu. "The progress of art," he said, "depends upon talent and not upon historical events. Goethe would have been the same great poet if there never had been a Frederick the Great, and the French Revolution, which surely was powerful enough in its workings, has not produced a single poet.''

Professor Auguste Ehrhard, the author of an admirable French work on Grillparzer, crowned by the French Academy, remarks that in a period of great literary unrest in Germany Grillparzer's æsthetic convictions never wavered. ''He was guided,'' says Ehrhard, ''by the artistic sense inherent in the Austrians, as well as by his own poetic instinct.'' His æsthetic education was of the broadest, and comprised a knowledge of music such as Sainte-Beuve and Lowell lacked, and Goethe never fully acquired. Goethe, indeed, was in his youth a performer of some skill on several musical instruments and sought in his old age, through his association with Zelter, to acquaint himself with certain musical theories, and Lowell recognised (in his essay on Pope) the value of music to a poet. ''Milton, Collins and Gray,'' he remarks, ''our three great masters of harmony, were all musicians.'' With Grillparzer, music was part of his very nature, and his familiarity with this art entered into all his æsthetic theories.

The extracts from Grillparzer's critical writings which appear in another part of this book will, to

some extent, give an idea of the comprehensiveness and originality of a critic whom Ehrhard
considers the greatest that Germany has produced
since the days of Lessing. As a characteristic
specimen of Grillparzer's breadth of view it will
suffice to point in this place to his appreciation of
Ghiberti, penned after reading a German translation of his *Chronicle of Florence:*

"I must confess that few books have made so
deep an impression upon me. While Benvenuto
Cellini's *Life* shows us the heaven-storming Titan,
who, intent upon his work in his inexhaustible
power, regards all those beside and around him as
so many disturbing and antagonising opponents,
Ghiberti's gentle, perhaps somewhat feminine,
nature clings with a glorifying love to his contemporaries, and affords us a picture of days
which had no equal in any other epoch in art.
The Michael-Angelo-like Brunelleschi, the joyous
Donatello, Masaccio, Filippo Lippi—monk and
painter—the wonderful Leonardo da Vinci, in
his early beginnings, and the peaceful painter of
Fiesole—briefly mentioned yet throwing over us,
as it were, a shimmer of his angelic halo—added
to all these a world of artists of the second and
third rank, whom we see not only in sharply defined outline, but in all their relations of life, and
in situations such as to-day are found only in

novels, but which those days produced in abundance—what an age! There are entire countries whose history from the creation of the world to the year of our Lord 1833 offers not half as much of real interest as little Florence under the Medici. Truly, he who espies at a distance an Italian in the street ought to uncover his head, and say to himself: 'Here is one of those who are the fathers of modern civilisation.' I do not doubt that many will ridicule such an idea. Let those not read Ghiberti's book; all others will enjoy it.''*

Grillparzer, like Goethe, capable of the highest imaginative flights, guarded with equal jealousy his critical independence. With all his admiration for Euripides, Lope, Shakespeare, and Goethe himself, he was, as it were, constantly on the guard against their overmastering power. When starting on a journey on one occasion, he asked himself: ''What books am I to take with me for my poetic flight? Little, and yet much! Herodotus and Plutarch, besides the two Spanish dramatists. And not Shakespeare? No, not Shakespeare, although he is perhaps the greatest product of the modern age. Not Shakespeare! He tyrannises over my intellect, and I want to remain free. I thank God that he exists, and that I have the good fortune to read him and re-read him, and absorb him. But now I shall try to forget him. The

ancients invigorate me, the Spaniards incite me
to productiveness; but the former are too remote,
the latter too purely human—with their blemishes
amid their greatest beauties, and their often exaggerated mannerisms—to influence deeply my
nature, my individual way of looking at things.
But the giant Shakespeare usurps the powers of
Nature, whose most magnificent mouth-piece he
was, and whosoever surrenders himself to him
will forever have to go to him for an answer to
any question which he may wish to ask Nature herself.''

SAINTE-BEUVE'S UNIQUE POSITION
IN LITERATURE

WITHIN the whole range of literature no country has produced a critic like Sainte-Beuve. He is unique in vastness of achievement, in the erudition and industry he brought to his task, as well as in the unfailing grace, apparently so spontaneous and yet the result of unremitting effort, which illumines his pages. French literature in its entirety lay open before him; he was at home with philosophers and journalists, with historians and scientists, with society and life in all their shades and, often enough, their shadows; with great and little men and women, with all prominent figures in the annals of French history; he analysed character as profoundly as he did books; and while he gave to France all the resources of an eminently French intellect, he spoke of her literature as one whose background was all literature, and who had assimilated the culture of the other great civilised nations.

Criticism was with Sainte-Beuve, as he himself said, "an instinct and a passion," but he laid down no critical canons, as other critics have done. Boileau and men of lesser eminence have attempted to teach what may be called the science of the profession, and Lessing has written an immortal text-book on one aspect of the subject. Sainte-Beuve embodied his critical views in countless articles, from which those who would learn his secret may deduce his theory as best they can. Yet he was lavish enough of direct advice, which no one who aspires to literary taste, let alone to literary judgment, can afford to ignore. We may open his pages anywhere, and we shall learn and admire. In one of his Monday *Causeries,* that on "Public Evening Readings" ("*Des Lectures Publiques du Soir,*" January 21, 1850), we seem to be initiated into a course of lectures not only on French literature and æsthetics, but on the proper study of literature in general, and on the art of reading wisely books of whatever kind. He speaks as the lover of French literature, who would open its treasures to his countrymen, and as the man of international culture who admires all that is of universal appeal. "I should wish," he warningly says, "the lecturer dwelling on the beauties and the grandeur of our literature and national history to guard against repeating what is so constantly said, in colleges and even in Academies on solemn occasions: that the French are the greatest and most sensible of all nations, and our literature the greatest of all literatures. I

should wish him to content himself with saying
that it is one of the finest, and that the world did
not begin and does not end with us."

Much as has been written about Sainte-Beuve,
his cosmopolitan aspect has not yet been sufficiently emphasised, although an attentive reading of his critical articles, whatever the subject,
cannot fail to disclose his international sympathies.   What he admires, for instance, above all
in Montaigne is that he "like Socrates, did not
consider himself citizen of a single town, but of
the whole world, that his imagination grasped, in
its wide sweep, the universal character of all ages
and all countries."   If he ranks Montaigne with
the wisest of Frenchmen, it is precisely because
he finds in him a wisdom that is not distinctively
French.   "Such as he is," says Sainte-Beuve,
"Montaigne is our Horace; he is like him in his
very nature and often in form and expression,
although in point of style he also resembles Seneca.
His book is a treasure-house of moral observations
and experiences; open his pages where we may,
and we shall be sure to find, no matter what his
momentary mood, some wise thought expressed in
a telling and impressive manner, something standing out in its beautiful and deep meaning, graven
permanently into one striking word, or a single
strong, intimate, or grand line."   The comparison

with Horace is carried further: we lose sight of Montaigne the Frenchman, and have before us once more the polished wit of antiquity, who bids us dismiss our private anxieties and public concerns, and refrain from borrowing trouble. Sainte-Beuve gives us a true measure of his critical capacity in such allusions as this. If we ask him for a full portrait of a literary critic of something of his own culture, a man after his own heart, he draws it for us in these words (*Nouveaux Lundis*, Vol. X, "Hommes et Dieux"):

"We have to inquire into the education of M. de Saint-Victor if we would make a real study of him, such as he deserves. His father was in his youth one of the most pleasing and most promising poets of the first Empire. His poetic translation of Anacreon is the work of a writer as scholarly as he is graceful. Had he continued in this strain, the Academy would certainly have opened its doors to him. Politics and the passions of the day withdrew him too soon from the exclusive cult of letters; but in the latter part of his life he sought consolation in the love of art, properly speaking, and became an expert judge of pictures. Young Saint-Victor, educated from early youth outside of France, first in Switzerland, afterwards in Italy—in Rome and other places full of living memories—soon learned to compare the master-

pieces of rival schools. He grew up with the idea
of the beautiful among the marbles and paintings
of the masters. It was given to him to see, like
Romeo, true beauty at an early age, and from that
day he could never more do without it. The
Italian culture deep within his soul determined his
future. One might have said that that young
man, when he came back to us, with his noble bearing, his pale profile, the play of his rather silent
and somewhat haughty lips, was a reincarnated
contemporary of the Capulets and Montagus.
He was a Venetian who had stepped out of a
portrait. Do not look for the Frenchman in him.
One often speaks thoughtlessly of the French
spirit and French humour, and endows with them
persons who cannot lay claim to them; Saint-
Victor, surely, has not a trace of this spirit; the
domestic pleasures of his first home have lost their
charm for him, and he sets no store by them; he
has seen better things in the world of the Medici
and the land of sunshine. His point of view is
different from ours, and the circle of his observation as expert or amateur far wider. Thus literary criticism restores its youth and freshness
through the accession of those French spirits that
have steeped themselves in other sources and, returning to us, transplant into our soil the taste for
new beauties and for intelligent comparisons."

Again and again this note of insistence on comparisons with other writers than those of one's own language is struck in Sainte-Beuve's writings. He would have the French profit by such critics as the Swiss De Muralt, who, in his *Lettres sur les Anglais et les Français,* tells Sainte-Beuve's countrymen certain wholesome truths. Apropos of De Muralt's criticism of Boileau's *Satires,* Sainte-Beuve remarks that such judgments are of particular value to those "who look at French literature at some distance, and take their standard of comparison from the great poets of all times and of all countries, and from human nature itself." With what convincing earnestness does Sainte-Beuve plead the cause of minor writers, like Gresset and Parny, who have been stripped by narrow critics of their peculiar charm and thus robbed of the appreciation due them. How ought one to approach writers like these? he asks. Are the learned but one-sided commentators to have it all their own dull way? What ought to be the proper equipment of the critic? "Is it necessary to adopt the method of Gervinus in order to understand and admire La Fontaine? In order to give to Gresset his proper place, to assign to an elegy of Parny the rank it deserves, is it indispensable for us to have gone the rounds of all literature, to have read the *Nibelungen* and to know by heart the mystic stanzas of Calderon?'' Possibly, he says. ''In any case, this is the longest route, and when we return home into our own quarters we run the risk of being so fatigued that we fall asleep. Nevertheless, I admit that if a small amount of knowledge takes us away from the love of beauty and simple charms, much knowledge brings us back to it.''

Sainte-Beuve looked upon spontaneous love of nature, truth, and beauty, as lying at the very foundation of the great works of literature, as of the great deeds of men. Against these sentiments the efforts of reformers beat in vain. If literature and all human institutions are to endure, it is because of their response to a universal need. The appeals of reformers to the intellect alone fail in literature, as they do in life. There is a significant passage on this subject in Sainte-Beuve's article on Sieyès. ''His mistake, like the mistakes of all who seek solitude, lay in believing that a radical reform in human nature is possible, and that man, even if we take the chosen few, can be made once for all to obey reason.''

Sainte-Beuve had as little of the zealous reformer and innovator in him as Goethe. They were alike in their distrust of apostles of any new creed, in their endeavour to preserve rather than to demolish and build anew. Sainte-Beuve's en-

tire activity as a critic breathes repose and moderation, and the past was ever present with him.
Genius without repose was to him incomplete and
incapable of perfection. He said of La Harpe
that he was wanting in some of the qualities essential in the formation of character, that he
had neither moderation nor balance, and did
not know what it means to stop at the right
time or to return wisely to one's moorings;
that he had no memory for the past. "The last
eleven or twelve years of his life," he remarked,
"showed that impossibility of his ever reaching
maturity which is the defect of certain emotional
natures."

What he liked, above all, in a writer was this
ability to pause and seek refuge from the petty
concerns of the moment in the permanent things
of the past. "Let there be," he said, in an article
on Jules Janin, "beyond the region of all the political systems and the borders of warring doc-
trines a territory more or less neutral—a kind of
sylvan retreat where one is welcome to stray for
a little while and dream of those things old as the
world and yet eternally young, of spring and
summer and love and youth; where one may even
walk about (if youth be past) with a book in one's
hand, and live with an author of another age, free
to enjoy him for the whole day, and, on returning

to the city, to ask every passer-by, 'Have you, too, read the book?' Monsieur Janin claims this right, and I claim it with him, although with less reason, for I have long since ceased to dream of youth and spring; but I do want the rambler and dreamer to have the right to read an old book, a book as far removed as possible from the quarrels of the day, and become completely absorbed in it.''

This art of dreaming, book in hand, Sainte-Beuve understood better than any critic before or after him. He finds himself in the company of another dreamer, Fontenelle, in his fanciful *Entretiens sur la Pluralité des Mondes* (talks on astronomy with a beautiful marquise in a beautiful park) and whither does Sainte-Beuve's fancy, spurred on by his vast knowledge, not lead him! While admitting the insinuating charm of these poetico-scientific discourses, he refuses to surrender to a method which "wheedles one into truth." How differently, he muses, does Pascal view Heaven and Nature! "Pascal felt in awe and trembling the majesty and immensity of Nature, while Fontenelle seems merely able to detect her cleverness. He never possessed that ideal, celestial geometry which a Pascal, a Dante, a Milton, or even a Buffon conceive of as established from the very beginning; he has it not and has no idea that he lacks it; he belittles the heavens in trying to explain them."

Sainte-Beuve was well read in the natural sciences; his study of medicine and anatomy in particular stood him in good stead, yet even in discussing men of science he was chiefly interested in the literary and personal aspects of his subject. He inquired into the range and depth of the author's mind, into his relations with the thinkers of other countries; he analysed his language, and asked whether his genius was imaginative and went hand in hand with grace and culture. Buffon, for this reason, interested him deeply; he found in him that "sacred fire" of genius which the great naturalist ignored in his dictum that genius is nothing but a matter of industry and patience. "The genius of Buffon," Sainte-Beuve said, "partakes equally of the poet and the philosopher; the two characters fuse and unite in him as was the case in primitive times." It has been said that Buffon oscillated between Newton and Descartes; Sainte-Beuve maintains that Buffon has an equal share, rather, in Newton and Milton, and that precisely where he is most systematic he is most poetic.

Sainte-Beuve let it be clearly understood that he wished to be ranged among the critics who, without promulgating a system of their own, prove by the manner in which they pronounce judgment their right to speak with authority. "The characteristic of critics in general," he said (in his article on Villemain and Cousin), "is, as the name indicates, to judge, and, wherever necessary, to render a clear-cut decision. Take all the important men to whom the title of critic has been applied, Malherbe, Boileau (for both were critics in the form of poets); Dr. Johnson in England, our own La Harpe, even De Fontanes—all these men, who were authoritative in their day, judged in matters of taste with vivacity, perhaps with too much dogmatism, but at all events clearly and with irresistible definiteness."

Constituted as he was, Sainte-Beuve demanded of the great writers, even in details, accurate knowledge. Vagueness was in his eyes an evidence, if not a confession, of weakness. He takes Balzac severely to task for his psychological vagaries, for his leanings towards the Swedenborgs, Mesmers, Saint-Germains and Cagliostros, and he makes effective use of his own physiological knowledge by twitting Balzac with having discovered, in his studies of the human anatomy, imaginary veins and lymphatic vessels.

Sainte-Beuve was not wholly just to Balzac, though he recognised in him "perhaps the most

original and penetrating painter of the morals of
his time." The immensity of his canvases, the
audaciousness of his attempts, offended his delicate sense of proportion, and he felt uneasy in the
morbid atmosphere of Balzac's characters. Sir
Walter Scott, too, as Sainte-Beuve recognised,
painted on a large scale, but he fills us with delight,
while Balzac, though he had come under his spell,
could only envy, but never emulate, the charm of
the Scotch wizard. "Had not Scott," asked
Sainte-Beuve, "breathed that universal charm,
that purity and healthfulness, that wholesome air
which circulates even amid the conflict of human
passions?" One feels the need of going to him
for refreshment, says Sainte-Beuve, of plunging
into some sane and clear book after finishing the
Parents Pauvres, or of immersing one's self in a
song of Milton, "in lucid streams," in those pure
currents of which the poet sings.

Sainte-Beuve speaks of English writers, not as
a Frenchman, but as Goethe speaks of Scott and
Goldsmith—with cosmopolitan understanding.
"If you knew English," he writes to a friend who
had sent him some verses of his own, "you would
have a treasure, upon which you could draw.
England has a poetic literature greatly superior
to ours—one which above all, is more healthful
and richer. Wordsworth has not been translated,

one cannot translate such things, one goes and
drinks them at the source.''

There are many allusions to Wordsworth in
Sainte-Beuve's pages, and he has himself felic-
itously translated—"imitated" the French call
it, with a just recognition of the limits of translation—several of Wordsworth's sonnets. Keats
also engaged Sainte-Beuve's muse at the time
when he still attempted poetic flights. He was,
however, more at home with the English prose
writers. He wrote penetrating essays on Gibbon,
Lord Chesterfield and Cowper, as he did on Benja-
min Franklin. They had in common a grace of
style not unlike his own, and in the case of Gibbon
the difficulty of defining a genius partly French
and yet characteristically British challenged
Sainte-Beuve's ingenuity. He was, however, in
all his criticisms impelled by a far higher motive
than zest in analysing style and character. He
possessed from the very beginning, says Paul
Elmer More, "that inquisitive passion for the
truth without which all other critical gifts are as
brass and tinkling cymbals." With such impassioned love of truth fondness for generalisation
is incompatible. Sainte-Beuve had an innate distrust for a certain class of historical writers whose
mission, almost as a matter of course, inclines
them to establish theories in order to explain facts.

Memoirs, the living testimony of eye-witnesses, he read with an enthusiasm which the sober pages of the historian seldom evoked. His admiration for Saint-Simon's pictures of the court of Louis XIV was unbounded, but he was sceptical as to the absolute value of Guizot's *Histoire de la Civilisation en Europe.* "Generalisations," he said, "which appear to us so profound when applied to distant ages, seem superficial enough if we apply them to our own time. Let me make my meaning clear: I admire that power of a broad and ingenious mind which remoulds and restores of the past all that can be restored, which gives to it, if not the true meaning, at least a plausible and probable meaning, which puts order into history, and gives direction and useful support to our study of it. But what I object to as dangerous is the tendency to draw conclusions from a past thus remade and reconstructed, from a past artificially simplified—conclusions bearing on a changeable and changing present. As for myself, after reading some of these high-sounding lessons on the History of Civilisation, given with so much precision and definiteness, I quickly open a volume of the Memoirs of Retz, in order to see the real play of human intrigue and masquerade."

There is a passage in Sainte-Beuve's article on Joubert (*Causeries du Lundi*, Vol. I, "Pensées,

Maximes et Correspondence de M. Joubert")
which gives us a glimpse of his method, if method
it can be called, of preserving intact his literary
detachment while nourishing his taste at the
varied sources of admirable writing.

"I have sometimes asked myself," he says,
"what a handbook of French rhetoric ought to
be, a book sensible, fair, and natural, and it has
even happened to me, once in my life, that I had
to talk on the subject before young people. What
was I to do to avoid falling into beaten tracks and
being caught by the fancies of the day? I began
simply with Pascal, with his thoughts on literature, in which the great writer laid down some of
his observations on his art. I read them aloud
and commented upon them. Then I took La
Bruyère's chapter on *Ouvrages de l'esprit*. I
then passed on to Fénelon's *Dialogues sur l'Élo-
quence* and his *Lettre à l'Académie Française;* I
went over the ground carefully, choosing my
points and always commenting by examples if
need be from living writers. Vauvenargues's
Thoughts and *Literary Characters* came next. I
borrowed from Voltaire the articles on Taste and
Style, in the *Dictionnaire Philosophique,* his
Temple of Taste, and some passages from the
letters in which he passes judgment on Boileau,
Racine and Corneille. I added, in order to widen

my horizon at this particular moment, some reflections on the intellect of Goethe and on English taste, as exemplified in Coleridge. Marmontel, in his *Élements de Littérature,* furnished me with an article on Style, an admirable piece of writing. I took good care not to omit Buffon on the same subject, whose words crowned the whole. Finally, with the classic circle complete, I gave my young hearers Joubert as a sort of dessert and choice tidbit. Here was a meal fit for Pythagoras!''

Who does not recognise, in the delicate play of Sainte-Beuve's fancy, the almost Spartan demands on himself which his conception of the duty of a critic imposed upon his time? Such a universal interest in literature, such conscientious preparation for the task before him, presupposed complete abstraction from society during the days of work. No one plodded more industriously than Sainte-Beuve, burying himself, as he did, among his books from morning till night, and only emerging on the one day intervening between the completion of one *Lundi* and the beginning of another. ''A critic,'' he said, ''ought not to have too many friends and social relations—those obligations dictated by convention. . . . Without being exactly freebooters, as we have been called, we must be able to roam about at will; we must have elbow-room. Monsieur Janin wittily said

one day to a lady who at an evening entertain-
ment introduced him to a number of guests: 'You
are procuring me so many friends that you
rob me of all my spirit.' ''

In a more serious vein, Sainte-Beuve insisted
that the critic must scrupulously weigh his words.
He must be sparing of superlatives and know the
value of perspective. In discussing M. de Saint-
Victor's critical manner, he said: ''The author's
preferences are expressed in an unmistakable
way. He observes proper gradation, and groups
literature and art as Raphael groups his School
of Athens and Ingres his ceilings. Each genius,
each talent, is placed according to its merits and
on its own plane: *Gil Blas* is not on a level with
Don Quixote.'' Sainte-Beuve had no patience
with the easy-going, complaisant critic who carries his optimism into literature, identifies himself
with no settled conviction, opposes no new movement, and, as critic, is all things to all men. He
acknowledged the exquisite good taste, in classic
matters, of that once famous critic Huet, but
he was repelled by the spineless amiability of
Huet's judgment concerning French literature.
''No doubt,'' he said, ''he was incomparably more
at home among the ancients than Boileau, who
indeed seemed almost an ignoramus beside him;
but of that keen literary feeling, that brisk move-

ment, that impetuous judgment that seem to spring from a glowing heart, Huet had not a particle." Sainte-Beuve discriminated very sharply between writers who merely adorn literature and the "thundering minds" that arouse a century. "It is after all," he says, "the ignorant, like Pascal, Descartes and Rousseau, men who have read little, but who think and dare, that, for good or evil, stir the world and make it move." Few of those men that have aroused a century appealed to Sainte-Beuve as much as Franklin, of whom, while dwelling on his lack of certain literary refinements, he said:

"Franklin is by nature above the anxieties of the Childe Harolds or the susceptibilities of the Chateaubriands. We, of the outspoken French race, might have wished that there had been something of all this in him. . . . Let us, however, look at Franklin such as he is, in his proper stature and in all his moral beauty. That judicious man, firm, astute, skilful, honest, remains unshaken when injustice approaches him or his compatriots. For many years he tries to enlighten public opinion in the mother country, and to avert extreme measures; until the last moment he does his utmost to bring about a reconciliation based on fairness; and when on the very eve of the final rupture, one of the influential men of England

[Lord Howe] leaves him still some hope of reconciliation, tears of joy roll down his cheeks. But when, finally, hardened injustice and obstinate pride close all avenues to his countrymen, he is carried away by the loftiest and most invincible passion, and he who thinks that *every peace is good* and that *every war is bad,* is henceforth for war, for the holy war of patriotic and legitimate defence.''

LOWELL, PATRIOT AND COSMO-POLITAN

LOWELL's fame as a critic has been overshadowed by his eminence in other fields, where public recognition is more easily obtained, or at least more spontaneously rendered. The range of his accomplishments was very wide. A poet whose Commemoration Ode stirred the heart of the nation to its depths, a brilliant satirist in prose and verse, a political writer of singular power, an admirable teacher and lecturer, a fascinating orator, conversationalist, and letter-writer, a skilful and dignified diplomat, and, above all, a pure and sagacious patriot—who would look, first and foremost, for the critic in so many-sided and picturesque a personality? Yet, the attentive reader of Lowell's works cannot fail to recognise that in all his activities—not seldom even in his poetry—the critical faculty was paramount. His ancestry amply accounts for his observant and reflective temperament, as it does for his love of Nature, especially in her rugged mood, his sympathy with the sturdy untutored man, racy of the soil, his hard-headed Yankee sense of humour.

In a famous distich Grillparzer, referring to

the beautiful hill that commands the finest view of Vienna, says: "If you look at the country around you from the heights of the Kahlenberg you will understand what I have written and what I am." Similarly, if we would know what Lowell was, and why he wrote as he did, we have to know New England and particularly Cambridge, where he was born and where he died. He was a man of the world, easily at home in the great capitals of Europe, but his musings ever took him back to the town on the Charles River. Puritan as he was in his sense of duty toward man and the State, his outlook on life and literature was that of the serene philosopher and the cosmopolitan critic. He disclaimed the title of scholar, but the extent of his reading was extraordinary, and his knowledge of both essentials and minutiæ in literary matters was deep and sound beyond that of most specialists. He drew inspiration from English, French, Italian, Spanish and German sources, as well as from the ancients. No critic of similar importance in literary history has spoken of the glories of the past with more contagious enthusiasm and with a freer fancy. He conducts us through the highways and byways of many literatures at a leisurely gait, and though his wilful digressions, his bewildering allusiveness, at times threaten to obstruct our path, we surrender ourselves with delight to so fascinating and instructive a guide.

The most important critical work of James Russell Lowell is not to be found in the book reviews which, as editor of the *Atlantic Monthly,* he contributed to its pages, though all his articles were scholarly criticism of a high order, sometimes seasoned with his characteristic wit. It is the essayist Lowell that gives us the measure of the critic.

Perhaps the ripest fruit of Lowell's learning and critical activity was his treatise on Dante— the outgrowth of that life-long familiarity with the poet of which Harvard students were to reap so rich a harvest; but it may be doubted whether this essay is to-day read with the same relish as his papers on lesser writers. He was most effective when least academic. Perhaps no other international critic is so quotable. His pages bristle with the unexpected—with sallies of wit and humour, puns of varying quality, curious metaphors and quaint conceits, with deep sentiment and shrewd wisdom. And the whole, if not always the last word in literary criticism, is itself delectable literature.

Posterity alone can decide whether the critic was also the prophet. In the case of Lowell, the best international judgment has already confirmed

his own in conspicuous instances. His estimate
of Carlyle has gradually superseded that extravagant eulogium which hailed in him the inspired
prophet of a new gospel in history and morals.
·Nothing more philosophic and, in the best sense of
the word, critical is likely to be written of Carlyle
than Lowell's words:

"Mr. Carlyle has an unequalled power and
vividness in painting detached scenes, in bringing
out in their full relief the oddities or peculiarities
of character; but he has a far feebler sense of
those gradual changes of opinion, that strange
communication of sympathy from mind to mind,
that subtle influence of very subordinate actors in
giving a direction to policy or action, which we
are wont somewhat vaguely to call the progress
of events. His scheme of history is purely an
epical one, where only leading figures appear by
name and are in any strict sense operative. He
has no conception of the people as anything else
than an element of mere brute force in political
problems, and would sniff scornfully at that un-
picturesque common-sense of the many which
comes slowly to its conclusions, no doubt, but compels obedience even from rulers the most despotic
when once its mind is made up. His history of
Frederick is, of course, a Fritiziad; but next to his
hero, the cane of the drill-sergeant and iron ram-

rods appear to be the conditions which to his mind satisfactorily account for the result of the Seven Years' War. It is our opinion, which subsequent events seem to justify, that, had there not been in the Prussian people a strong instinct of nationality, Protestant nationality too, and an intimate conviction of its advantages, the war might have ended quite .otherwise. Frederick II left the machine of war which he received from his father even more perfect than he found it, yet within a few years of his death it went to pieces before the shock of French armies animated by an idea. Again a few years, and the Prussian soldiery, inspired once more by the old national fervour, were victorious. After all, is it not moral forces that make the heaviest battalions, other things being tolerably equal? Were it not for the purely picturesque bias of Mr. Carlyle's genius, for the necessity which his epical treatment lays upon him of always having a protagonist, we should be astonished that an idealist like him should have so little faith in ideas and so much in matter.''

As in the case of other great humourists, the reader is sometimes apt to overlook Lowell's penetrating sagacity while admiring the pungency of his wit; and the very appositeness of his metaphors tends to obscure their critical value. Yet, can humour be turned to juster critical account than in such a passage as this:

"Since *Sartor Resartus* Mr. Carlyle has done little but repeat himself with increasing emphasis and heightened shrillness. Warning has steadily heated toward denunciation, and remonstrance soured toward scolding. The image of the Tartar prayer-mill, which he borrowed from Richter and turned to such humorous purpose, might be applied to himself. The same phrase comes round and round, only the machine, being a little crankier, rattles more, and the performer is called on for a more visible exertion. If there be not something very like cant in Mr. Carlyle's later writings, then cant is not the repetition of a creed after it has become a phrase by the cooling of that white-hot conviction which once made it both the light and warmth of the soul. I do not mean intentional and deliberate cant, but neither is that which Mr. Carlyle denounces so energetically in his fellowmen of that conscious kind. I do not mean to blame him for it, but mention it rather as an interesting phenomenon of human nature. The stock of ideas which mankind has to work with is very limited, like the alphabet, and can at best have an air of freshness given it by new arrangements and combinations, or by application to new times and circumstances. Montaigne is but Ecclesiastes writing in the sixteenth century, Voltaire but Lucian in the eighteenth. Yet both are original, and so certainly is Mr. Carlyle, whose borrowing is mainly from his own former works. But he does this so often and so openly, that we may at least be sure that he ceased growing a number of years ago, and is a remarkable example of arrested development.

"The cynicism, however, which has now become the prevailing temper of his mind, has gone on expanding with unhappy vigour. In Mr. Carlyle it is not, certainly, as in Swift, the result of personal disappointment, and of the fatal eye of an accomplice for the mean qualities by which power could be attained that it might be used for purposes as mean. It seems rather the natural corruption of his exuberant humour. Humour in its first analysis is a perception of the incongruous, and in its highest development, of the incongruity between the actual and the ideal in men and life. With so keen a sense of the ludicrous contrast between what men might be, nay, wish to be, and what they are, and with a vehement nature that demands the instant realisation of his vision of a world altogether heroic, it is no wonder that Mr. Carlyle, always hoping for a thing and always disappointed, should become bitter. Perhaps if he expected less he would find more. Saul seeking

his father's asses found himself turned suddenly
into a king; but Mr. Carlyle, on the lookout for a
king, always seems to find the other sort of
animal.''

Almost every page that Lowell wrote bears
proof of his love of letters, his gusto in borrowing
from a half-forgotten author, no matter in what
language. Unsystematic, on the whole, his reading undeniably was. One of his most discrimi-
nating critics, Mr. Ferris Greenslet, well says of
him: "Lowell, it is needless to say at this hour,
was never quite a scholar in the German sense of
the word, nor even in the modern American academic sense: but he was a scholar in what we may
perhaps think a more admirable sense—that in
which the bookmen of the Renaissance were so."
Yet there were at least two foreign fields, besides
Dante literature, in which Lowell was thoroughly
at home: French language and literature of the
ante-classic period, and the dramas of Calderon.
Though he entered upon his post of American
Minister to Spain with a comprehensive knowledge
of Spanish literature, and a mastery of the language which soon procured him admission to the
Spanish Academy, it was only to Calderon, and
next to him to Cervantes, that he gave his heart.
He revelled in Calderon as Grillparzer did in
Lope. Allusions to Calderon give point to not

a few of Lowell's critical remarks; and they may come upon us, with his startling suddenness, in the most unexpected places. While on the ocean, he says: "When we were up with the Azores, we began to meet flying-fish and Portuguese men-of-war beautiful as the galley of Cleopatra, tiny craft that dared these seas before Columbus. I have seen one of the former rise from the crest of a wave, and, glancing from another some two hundred feet beyond, take a fresh flight of perhaps as far. How Calderon would have similised this pretty creature had he ever seen it! How would he have run him up and down the gamut of simile! If a fish, then a fish with wings; if a bird, then a bird, with fins; and so on, keeping up the light shuttle-cock of a conceit as is his wont."

Unconsciously, Lowell, in dwelling on Calderon's hunt for similes, has described the bent of his own mind. The Spanish dramatist is to him one of the great writers of all time. "For fascination of style and profound suggestion, it would be hard to name another author superior to Calderon, if indeed equal to him. His charm was equally felt by two minds as unlike each other as those of Goethe and Shelley. These in themselves are sufficient achievements, and the intellectual life of a nation could maintain itself on the unearned increment of these without further addition to its resources."

One of the most distinctive characteristics of Lowell's critical genius is the possession of a robust common sense—"horse sense" the colloquial phrase has termed it—which accompanied his cosmopolitan standards and in no way jars with his lofty idealism. No one has written with greater admiration of Emerson than he. Transcendentalism, as personified in Emerson and illumined in his pages, was to him one thing; transcendentalism as lived by Thoreau and expounded by the lesser lights of New England, was quite another. There was need, in Lowell's day, for such a critical clearing of the atmosphere as this in the article on Thoreau, written in 1865:

"What contemporary, if he was in the fighting period of his life (since Nature sets limits about her conscription for spiritual fields, as the state does in physical warfare), will ever forget what was somewhat vaguely called the 'Transcendental Movement' of thirty years ago? Apparently set astir by Carlyle's essays on the 'Signs of the Times,' and on 'History,' the final and more immediate impulse seemed to be given by *Sartor Resartus*. At least the republication in Boston of that wonderful Abraham à Sancta Clara sermon on Falstaff's text of the miserable forked radish gave the signal for a sudden mental and moral mutiny. *Ecce nunc tempus acceptabile!* was shouted on all hands with every variety of emphasis, and by voices of every conceivable pitch, representing the three sexes of men, women, and Lady Mary Wortley Montagus. The nameless eagle of the tree Ygdrasil was about to sit at last, and wild-eyed enthusiasts rushed from all sides, each eager to thrust under the mystic bird that chalk egg from which the new and fairer Creation was to be hatched in due time. *Redeunt Saturnia regna,*— so far was certain, though in what shape, or by what methods, was still a matter of debate. Every possible form of intellectual and physical dyspepsia brought forth its gospel. Bran had its prophets, and the presartorial simplicity of Adam its martyrs, tailored impromptu from the tar-pot by incensed neighbours, and sent forth to illustrate the 'feathered Mercury,' as defined by Webster and Worcester. Plainness of speech was carried to a pitch that would have taken away the breath of George Fox; and even swearing had its evangelists, who answered a simple inquiry after their health with an elaborate ingenuity of imprecation that might have been honourably mentioned by Marlborough in general orders. Everybody had a mission (with a capital M) to attend to everybody-else's business. No brain but had its private maggot, which must have found pitiably short commons sometimes. Not a few impecunious zealots abjured the use of money (unless earned by other people), professing to live on the internal revenues of the spirit. Some had an assurance of instant millennium so soon as hooks and eyes should be substituted for buttons. Communities were established where everything was to be common but common-sense. Men renounced their old gods, and hesitated only whether to bestow their furloughed allegiance on Thor or Budh.''

Thus the satire rambles on, with a fling at the ''foreign revolutionists out of work,'' who added to the general confusion of tongues in broken English, and a note of regret that the comic side of the affair could be barely hinted at, so endless was the material. The word ''transcendental,'' we are told, was then ''the maid of all work for those who could not think.'' In a more serious vein, Lowell continues:

''The truth is, that there was a much nearer metaphysical relation and a much more distant æsthetic and literary relation between Carlyle and the Apostles of the Newness, as they were called in New England, than has commonly been supposed. Both represented the reaction and revolt against *Philisterei*, a renewal of the old battle begun in modern times by Erasmus and Reuchlin, and continued by Lessing, Goethe, and, in a far narrower sense, by Heine in Germany, and of which Fielding, Sterne, and Wordsworth in different ways have been the leaders in England. It was simply a struggle for fresh air, in which, if the windows could not be opened, there was danger that panes would be broken, though painted with images of saints and martyrs. Light, coloured by these reverend effigies, was none the more respirable for being picturesque. There is only one thing better than tradition, and that is the original and eternal life out of which all tradition takes its rise. It was this life which the reformers demanded, with more or less clearness of consciousness and expression, life in politics, life in literature, life in religion.''

Emerson, as Lowell wittily says, ''kept aloof from active partnership in these movements of reform, but was the sleeping partner who supplied a great part of their capital. The artistic range of Emerson is narrow, as every well-read critic must feel at once; and so is that of Æschylus, so is that of Dante, so is that of Montaigne, so is that of Schiller, so is that of nearly every one except Shakespeare; but there is a gauge of height no less than of breadth, of individuality as well as of comprehensiveness, and, above all, there is the standard of genetic power, the test of the masculine as distinguished from the receptive minds. There are staminate plants in literature, that make no fine show of fruit, but without whose pollen, quintessence of fructifying gold, the garden had been barren. Emerson's mind is emphatically one of these, and there is no man to whom our æsthetic culture owes so much. The Puritan revolt had made us ecclesiastically and the Revolution politically independent, but we were still socially and intellectually moored to English thought, till Emerson cut the cable and gave us a chance at the dangers and the glories of blue water. No man young enough to have felt it can forget or cease to be grateful for the mental and moral *nudge* which he received from the writings of his high-minded and brave-spirited countryman. That we agree with him, or that he always agrees with himself, is aside from the question; but that he arouses in us something that we are the better for having awakened, whether that something be of opposition or assent, that he speaks always to what is highest and least selfish in us, few Americans of the generation younger than his own would be disposed to deny. His oration before the Phi Beta Kappa Society at Cambridge, some thirty years ago, was an event without any former parallel in our literary annals, a scene to be always treasured in the memory for its picturesqueness and its inspiration. What crowded and breathless aisles, what windows clustering with eager heads, what enthusiasm of approval, what grim silence of foregone dissent! It was our Yankee version of a lecture by Abélard, our Harvard parallel to the last public appearances of Schelling.''

Lowell, though fond of the great classic writers and never long separated from his Homer and Euripides, has been charged with indifference to Hellenism. There is certainly no evidence that he arrogated to himself the right to speak authoritatively on matters of classic art; but we cannot fail to recognise that he was as deeply imbued with the classic spirit as Goethe, Grillparzer, and Sainte-Beuve. He distinguished acutely between the conflicting claims of classicists and modernists, pleading, as we shall see later on, for the moderns, but not as against the ancients. In his article on Lessing, he says: ''It is true that Machiavelli was the first to write with classic pith and point in a living language; but he is, for all that, properly an ancient. Montaigne is really the first modern writer,—the first who assimilated his Greek and Latin, and showed that an author might be original and charming, even classical, if he did not try too hard. He is also the first modern critic, and his judgments of the writers of antiquity are

those of an equal. He made the ancients his serv-
ants, to help him think in Gascon French; and, in
spite of his endless quotations, began the crusade
against pedantry. It was not, however, till a century later, that the reform became complete in
France, and then crossed the Channel. Milton is
still a pedant in his prose, and not seldom even in
his great poem. Dryden was the first Englishman who wrote perfectly easy prose, and he owed
his style and turn of thought to his French reading. His learning sits easily on him, and has a
modern cut."

Lowell, like every other great critic, had his own
method; his discursiveness, his playful seriousness, the interfusion of the classic and the modern,
the Gallic and the Puritan spirit, are all part of
his charm. But he could stick to his text as
closely as any parson (indeed he often moralised
as well as any), and it is precisely when he speaks
on Greek art and the Greek drama that his argument is most closely-knit and serious. In his essay on Dante he says:

"Greek art at its highest point is doubtless the
most perfect that we know. But its circle of motives was essentially limited; and the Greek drama
in its passion, its pathos, and its humour is primarily Greek, and secondarily human. Its tragedy
chooses its actors from certain heroic families,

and finds its springs of pity and terror in physical suffering and worldly misfortune. Its best
examples, like the *Antigone,* illustrate a single
duty, or, like the *Hippolytus,* a single passion, on
which, as on a pivot, the chief character, statu-
esquely simple in its details, revolves as pieces of
sculpture are sometimes made to do, displaying
its different sides in one invariable light. The
general impression left on the mind (and this is
apt to be a truer one than any drawn from single
examples) is that the duty is one which is owed
to custom, that the passion leads to a breach of
some convention settled by common consent, and
accordingly it is an outraged society whose figure looms in the background, rather than an offended God. At most it was one god of many,
and meanwhile another might be friendly. In
the Greek epic, the gods are partisans, they hold
caucuses, they lobby and log-roll for their candi-
dates. The tacit admission of a revealed code of
morals wrought a great change. The complexity
and range of passion is vastly increased when the
offence is at once both crime and sin, a wrong
done against order and against conscience at the
same time. The relation of the Greek tragedy to
the higher powers is chiefly antagonistic, struggle
against an implacable destiny, sublime struggle,
and of heroes, but sure of defeat at last. And

that defeat is final. Grand figures are those it
exhibits to us, in some respects unequalled, and in
their severe simplicity they compare with modern
poetry as sculpture with painting. Considered
merely as works of art, these products of the
Greek imagination satisfy our highest conception
of form. They suggest inevitably a feeling of
perfect completeness, isolation, and independence,
of something rounded and finished in itself. The
secret of those old shapers died with them; their
wand is broken, their book sunk deeper than ever
plummet sounded. The type of their work is the
Greek temple, which leaves nothing to hope for
in unity and perfection of design, in harmony and
subordination of parts, and in entireness of impression. But in this æsthetic completeness it
ends. It rests solidly and complacently on the
earth, and the mind rests there with it.''

In discussing Swinburne's Tragedies Lowell re-
fers to the old dispute as to the comparative
merits of the ancients and the moderns which far
antedates Fontenelle's days, when it reached
fever-heat. Like Sainte-Beuve, who, with all his
admiration for the classics, ridicules those who
cannot think without their permission, Lowell
did his own thinking, after enjoying the best
thought that ancients and moderns could offer
him. That we neither honour the ancients nor

profit ourselves by lifeless imitation of classic literature, Lowell shows in his own striking way, in the same essay: "Men still pain themselves to write Latin verses, matching their wooden bits of phrase together as children do dissected maps, and measuring the value of what they have done, not by any standard of intrinsic merit, but by the difficulty of doing it. Petrarch expected to be known to posterity by his Africa. Gray hoped to make a Latin poem his monument. Goethe, who was classic in the only way it is now possible to be classic, in his *Hermann and Dorothea,* and at least Propertian in his *Roman Idylls,* wasted his time and thwarted his creative energy on the mechanical mock-antique of an unreadable *Achilleis.*"

As in the case of Sainte-Beuve, we have to know all that Lowell said of Goethe in order to concede that the occasional strictures of a foreign critic concerning the great German do not necessarily involve the crime of sacrilege. Lowell was even more outspoken in what he said of Lessing. Stahr's Life of Lessing served him as a text—one might say a pretext—for a homily on the heaviness of German style, and there is too much merciless dissection of the luckless biographer to enable Lowell to do full justice to his hero; but if the looseness of structure disturbs the symmetry of the essay, the witty digressions certainly illumine

and adorn it. Lowell was not lacking in due appreciation of Lessing; he admired, perhaps, no
other character in literature more fully, but he did
not find in him an unfailing source of inspiration,
as he did in Dante, Cervantes or, most of all possibly, in the old English dramatists and poets.
Chaucer, Dryden, Marlowe, Chapman, Beaumont
and Fletcher, Massinger and Ford—how lovingly
he dwelt on them, what life and colour they all
assumed in his hands, what rich mines of critical
suggestions and comparisons he opens up to us in
his glowing pages! They had nourished his
youth, and he returned to them in old age, his
unforgetable early New England impressions enriched by all that old England had been to him
during his honoured residence there. Nor had
any American Minister ever given to England
what James Russell Lowell could give while representing his country at the Court of St. James.
The quiet Harvard scholar at once took rank not
only with famous old-world scholars and littéra-
teurs, with ripe diplomats and statesmen, but with
the most accomplished orators and conversational-
ists, all the impressive personalities that graced
the best of London society.

It is not too much to say that his addresses at
the numerous public functions to which he will-
ingly lent the never-failing charm, of his presence

marked an era in the intercourse between the two countries. English philosophers and workingmen alike listened spellbound to the message of the American Minister, who, on assuming the presidency of the Birmingham and Midland Institute, expounded to the old world the meaning of "Democracy" in the new; the literary societies of London asked themselves who of their number could speak of Fielding or Coleridge with a deeper appreciation of the treasures of English literature, and temper criticism with such matchless grace. How deftly he mingles, in his address at the unveiling of the bust of Fielding, praise of the great novelist with denunciation of that British Philistinism which hesitates, on moral grounds, to recognise his excellence. "Fielding," he said, "needs no recognition from us; his fame is established and admitted, and his character is gradually clearing itself of the stains with which malice or jealousy or careless hearsay had darkened it. It has become an established principle of criticism that in judging a man we must take into account the age in which he lived, and which was as truly a part of him as he of it. Fielding's genius has drawn forth the sympathetic commendation of such widely different men as Gibbon, Scott, Coleridge, Thackeray, and Leslie Stephen, and of such a woman as George Eliot.

. . . The dramatic pieces that he wrote during his early period were, it is true, shamefully gross, though there are humorous hints in them that have been profitably worked up by later writers; but what strikes me most in them is that there is so little real knowledge of life, the result of personal experience, and that the social scenery and conception of character are mainly borrowed from his immediate predecessors, the dramatists of the Restoration. In grossness his plays could not outdo those of Dryden, whose bust has stood so long without protest in Westminster Abbey. As to any harm they can do there is little to be apprehended, for they are mostly as hard to read as a Shapira manuscript. I do not deny that Fielding's temperament was far from being over nice. I am willing to admit, if you will, that the woof of his nature was coarse and animal. I should not stop short of saying that it was sensual. Yet he liked and admired the highest and best things of his time—the art of Hogarth, the acting of Garrick, the verse of Pope. He is said indeed to have loved low company, but his nature was so companionable and his hunger for knowledge so keen, that I fancy he would like any society that was not dull, and any conversation, however illiterate, from which he could learn anything to his purpose. It may be suspected that the polite conversation of the men of that day would differ little, except in grammar, from the talk of the pothouse.''

With all the freedom of the accredited Minister of the great modern Republic and of the ancient Republic of Letters, Lowell lashed those critics who would read a Fielding out of polite literature because of his offences against polite society. Himself endowed with that penetrating mother wit which goes to the root of things, Lowell possessed in equal degree the gift of imagination, without which all the other qualifications of the critic go for naught.   In his address on Coleridge he embodied what may be considered his ideal of the critic's equipment.

''He certainly was a main influence in showing the English mind how it could emancipate itself from the vulgarising tyranny of common sense, and teaching it to recognise in the imagination an important factor not only in the happiness but in the destiny of man.   In criticism he was, indeed, a teacher and interpreter whose service was incalculable.   He owed much to Lessing, something to Schiller, and more to the younger Schlegel, but he owed most to his own sympathetic and penetrative imagination.   This was the lifted torch (to borrow his own words again) that bade the starry walls of passages, dark before to the apprehen-

sion of even the most intelligent reader, sparkle
with a lustre, latent in them to be sure, but not all
their own. As Johnson said of Burke, he wound
into his subject like a serpent. His analysis was
elucidative mainly, if you will, but could not have
been so except in virtue of the processes of con-
structive and philosophical criticism that had gone
on so long in his mind as to make its subtle apprehension seem an instinct. As he was the first
to observe some of the sky's appearances and
some of the shyer revelations of outward nature,
so he was also first in noting some of the more oc-
cult phenomena of thought and emotion. It is a
criticism of parts and passages, and was scattered
carelessly in *obiter dicta,* but it was not a bringing of the brick as a specimen of the whole house.
It was comparative anatomy, far rather, which
from a single bone reconstructs the entire living
organism. Many of his hints and suggestions are
more pregnant than whole treatises, as where he
says that the wit of Hudibras is the wit of thought.
But what I think constitutes his great power, as
it certainly is his greatest charm, is the perpetual
presence of imagination, as constant a quality
with him as fancy is with Calderon. She was his
lifelong housemate, if not always hanging over
his shoulders and whispering in his ear, yet within
easy call, like the Abra of Prior—

" 'Abra was with him ere he spoke her name,
    And if he called another, Abra came.' "

There is a curious antagonism between Lowell's
aversion to pedantic display of learning and the
profusion of antiquarian lore in his own pages.
"I am by temperament impatient of detail in com-
municating what I have acquired," he says in the
Prefatory Note to his Essays, "and too often put
into a parenthesis or a note conclusions arrived at
by long study and reflection." He was indeed as
lavish of such condensed wisdom as Sainte-
Beuve, and he appreciated brevity and directness
in others perhaps even more than the French
critic. He realised that "simplicity, where it is
not a careless gift of the Muses, is the last and
most painful achievement of conscientious self-
denial." He had a loving partiality for the leisurely pace of an Izaak Walton, but biographical
amplitude in the case of lesser lights found no
favour in his eyes. "Biography," he amusingly
said, "has found out a process by which what is
human may be so thrust upon as to become inhuman." Here again, as so often in criticising
the moderns, he holds up the ancients as a model.
"Plutarch, a man of the most many-sided moral
and intellectual interests, has a truer sense of
proportion, and tempers his amiable discursive-

ness with an eye to his neighbour's dial.   And in his case the very names of his heroes are mostly so trumpet-like as both to waken attention and to warrant it, ushering in the bearers of them like that *flourish* on the Elizabethan stage which told that a king was coming.''

The kings in literature alone occupied Lowell's mind permanently, as they did the minds of the other great critics of whom we have spoken.   Like them, when weary of the petty concerns of the day, he returns to the ancients and their golden age, which his fancy so often contrasts with the baser metal of our modern epoch.   ''I have my own suspicion sometimes,'' he muses, ''that the true age of flint is before and not behind us. . . . The siege of Troy will be remembered when those of Vicksburg and Paris are forgotten.''

GOETHE, GRILLPARZER, SAINTE-
BEUVE AND LOWELL ON
COMMON GROUND

GOETHE ON THE CAMPAGNA

(From a painting by Tischbein)

ENGLISH LITERATURE

GOETHE ON MELANCHOLY IN ENGLISH POETS

THE quiet enjoyment of life is based upon the regular recurrence of the things about us. The alternation of night and day, of the seasons, of blossoms and fruit, and of all else that comes to us periodically for our pleasure—these give life its real zest. The more we open our hearts to these enjoyments the happier we are; but if these phenomena come and go without our taking any interest in them, if we become insensitive to their charms, then the most serious of all evils, the gravest of all maladies, seizes us, and life becomes an intolerable burden. There is a story of an Englishman who hanged himself because he was tired of dressing and undressing himself daily. I knew myself a gardener, a worthy man, in charge of an extensive park, who once exclaimed in disgust: "Must I always see these rain clouds move from west to east?" Of one of our most eminent men it is related that he expressed his vexation at seeing spring always return in its green garb, and wished it might for once appear in red. These are real symptoms of weariness of life, which so frequently result in suicide, and these symptoms show themselves in persons of a reflective and self-absorbed nature more often than one would imagine.

Nothing produces this weariness of life more frequently than the recurrence of the passion of love. The first love, it is rightly said, is the only one; for in and through the second, the highest meaning of love is lost. The conception of the eternal and infinite which elevates and supports it is destroyed, and it appears transitory like everything that has its recurrence. The conflict between sensuality and morals, which separates in this complex and cultivated age the sensations of love and desire, leads in such cases to an exaggeration of which no good can come.

A young man, moreover, easily perceives, if not in himself, at least in others, that there are periodic changes in the world of morals as there are in the seasons. The condescension of the great, the favour of the mighty, the stimulus of the active, the friendliness of the masses, the attachment of an individual—all this comes and goes and can be as little regulated by us as can the sun, the moon and the stars. And yet these are not things that change in the course of nature, they vanish through our own fault or that of others, by accident or fate; but change they do, and we are never sure of them.

But what causes a sensitive youth more uneasiness than anything else is the constant recurrence of his faults; for long, indeed, it takes us to perceive that, while developing our virtues, we simultaneously cultivate our failings. The former are rooted in the latter, and our secret faults branch out in all their strength and variety as surely as do our virtues in the open day. But since we generally practise our virtues consciously and with full purpose, while we are unconsciously surprised by our faults, the former rarely give us any pleasure, while the latter constantly give us trouble and pain. Herein lies the great difficulty, indeed almost the impossibility, of arriving at self-knowledge. Given, then, a youth whose blood boils within him, whose power of imagination is easily paralysed, now by one influence, now by another, who finds himself amid the uncertain movements of the passing day, and we shall not wonder at his restless efforts to free himself from all his entanglements.

But all these melancholy reflections, which lead those who give themselves up to them into endless paths, could not have found so favourable a soil in the minds of German youths had not an occasion from without urged them on in their sad pursuit.

They found such an incitement in the works of English literature, particularly in English poetry, whose great excellences are joined to a sad seriousness, which imparts itself to whoever reads it. The thinking Briton is surrounded from early youth by a stirring and active world, which stimulates all the ability he possesses; sooner or later he finds that he must gather all his wits if he is to do justice to it. How many English poets have in their youth led a loose and riotous life and early thought themselves justified in complaining of the vanity of all earthly things! How many have tried their hand at great affairs and played a part, important or unimportant, in parliament, at court, in the cabinet or in an embassy, or have participated in internal commotions, national and governmental changes, only to gain, more often than not, disagreeable experiences either concerning themselves or their friends and patrons! How many have been exiled, driven from home, imprisoned and deprived of their possessions!

Merely to be a spectator of such great events inspires serious thought, and constant seriousness leads to reflections on the transitoriness and vanity of all human things. The Germans, too, are a serious nation, and therefore English poetry appeals to them greatly, impressing them with its loftier origin. English poetry is the outcome of great and able minds, versed in the ways of the world, of tender and deep emotions, a firm will, and intense energy—the noblest qualities that men of intellect and culture can possess.   But all these together do not make a poet.   True poetry, a worldly gospel, announces its presence by diffusing an inward serenity and outward sense of enjoyment that free us from the oppression of earthly cares.   Like an airship it lifts us, together with our ballast, into higher regions, leaving the confused mazes of this earth below us in a bird's-eye view.   The gayest and the most serious works have but the same purpose: to temper by skilful and natural description both sorrow and gaiety. Looked at in this way, most English poems, generally of a didactic and moralising nature, betray a gloomy weariness of life.   Not only Youngs' *Night Thoughts*, where this theme had been admirably worked out, but all the other meditative poems stray imperceptibly into this melancholy region, where the mind has to grapple with a problem which it is unable to solve, since the recourse to religion, however scant, is lacking.   One might print volumes as a commentary on the terrible text:

> Then old Age and Experience, hand in hand,
> Lead him to death, and make him understand,

After a search so painful and so long,
That all his life he has been in the wrong.

What lends the finishing touch to the misanthropy of English poets, and taints their writings with that unpleasant sensation of general discontent, is the fact that the many dissensions of the British commonwealth compel them to devote, if not their entire life, at least much of it, to one party or another. A writer of this kind cannot praise or defend the cause he has espoused or those to whom he is attached without exciting envy and hostility, and thus he exercises his talent in speaking as ill as possible of his opponents, and in adding as much point and venom as he can to his satirical weapons. If this is done by both parties, the world that lies between them wholly disappears from our view, so that, to speak mildly, a great people whose actions we know to be sensible appears in poetry to be given up to nothing but folly and madness. Even the poems that breathe the tenderest affection deal with the saddest subjects. In one of these there dies a forsaken maiden, in another a faithful lover is drowned, or before he can reach his lady love, as he rashly tries to swim ashore, he is devoured by a shark; and thus when a poet like Gray settles down in a country churchyard, and harps upon.

the old familiar strings, he may count upon
gathering around him a large number of those who
love melancholy. Milton, in his *Allegro,* must
first, in impassioned verse, chase away melancholy before he can attain to a very moderate degree of joy, and even cheerful Goldsmith loses
himself in elegy-like strains as he pictures to us,
with the saddest charms, in his *Deserted Village,*
that lost paradise which his *Traveller* vainly
seeks to regain in roaming over the whole world.
—*Autobiography,* Part III, Book XIII.

GOETHE ON GOLDSMITH

A Protestant country parson is perhaps the
most beautiful subject for a modern idyll; like
Melchizedek he stands before us, both priest and
king. He is connected with the most innocent of
all earthly states, that of the husbandman, connected by similarity of occupation and similar
family relations. He is father, head of the family, tiller of the soil—an ideal member of the community. His higher calling rests on this pure,
beautiful, terrestrial basis. His task is to guide
men throughout life, to minister to their intellectual development, to give them his blessing at
the principal epochs in their lives, to instruct,
strengthen, and console them, and where the present admits of no consolation, to point to the hope,

nay certainty, of a happy future. Imagine such a man, so strong in the purity of his sentiments and convictions as to remain unshaken under all circumstances, and thereby alone elevated above the multitude, from whom such purity and firmness cannot be expected; endow him with the learning requisite for his profession, behold him cheerfully and uniformly active, even passionately so, since he never neglects for a single moment any opportunity of doing good—take all this for granted, and you have indeed a well-equipped man. And if at the same time we add a certain narrowness necessary, not only to keep him contented within his limited sphere, but to make him willing, in case of need, to exchange it for a still more limited one; if we find him possessed of a kindly, forgiving, resolute nature and of other praiseworthy traits in keeping with such a character, and see in him beyond all this a yielding and cheerful spirit, tolerating smilingly his own failings and those of others—we have before us a fair portrait of our excellent Vicar of Wakefield.—*Autobiography,* Part II, Book X.

GOETHE ON WALTER SCOTT

We find in Walter Scott's descriptions everywhere the firmest grasp and the greatest accuracy —the result of his comprehensive knowledge of

the world, obtained by life-long study and observation and daily discussion of important events.
And how great is his talent, how wide and deep
are his interests! You remember the English
critic who compared poets with singers, some of
whom command but a few notes, while others have
voices of the largest compass and command
equally high and low notes. Walter Scott is of
the latter kind. There is in his *Fair Maid of
Perth* not a single weak passage to remind you
that there are limits to his talent and his knowledge. He is a perfect master of his subject in
every direction. The king, his royal brother, the
heir to the throne, the head of the clergy, the
nobles, the magistrates, citizens and artisans, the
Highlanders,—all are drawn with the same firm
hand and depicted with equal truth.—*Eckermann's
Conversations with Goethe.*

GRILLPARZER ON WALTER SCOTT
1823

Critics have gone so far as to compare Walter
Scott with Shakespeare, and indeed to put them on
the same level. Anything more absurd it would
be difficult to imagine. Precisely those features
wherein they are supposed to be akin, their ways
of drawing characters, show a colossal difference.
All of Shakespeare's characters are full of pulsat-

ing life, marvellously conceived by one who had
the most penetrating eye for the inner workings of
human nature; they all develop in accordance with
the laws of their individuality. They reconcile
us even to their apparent contradictions by the
sheer power of their actuality. Shakespeare did
not endow his persons with character, they pre-
sented themselves to him fully equipped and perfectly individualised. Scott *makes* characters,
sometimes successfully, sometimes less so, but the
will to create is always there, and even where his
characters display their most striking traits the
intention is only too obvious. He is a keen observer, and what he has observed he can describe
vividly and skilfully, but each of his characters
consists, closely considered, of a variety of traits
which his mastering intellect has formed into a
whole. With Shakespeare, on the other hand,
everything proceeds from the unity of the inner
conception, which branches out into a multitude of
seemingly contradictory peculiarities. What can
be achieved by knowledge of the world and of
mankind, by the study of history and psychology,
by power of observation and keen intellect, Scott
has in abundance, and it is his glory that this is
so. But the real central interest, the inexplicable
vital principle, these are lacking in his characters,
and in this respect he cannot be said to occupy a

very high rank among writers. The persons in his stories have therefore a distinct character only as long as he describes them, as long as they are in repose, as long as he talks of them; as soon as they begin to act, the whole elaborate structure seems to totter, and they betray more and more clearly that they were born of the intellectual effort of their author.

LOWELL ON WALTER SCOTT.

I

I can conceive of no healthier reading for a boy, or girl either, than Scott's novels, or Cooper's, to speak only of the dead. I have found them very good reading at least for one young man, for one middle-aged man, and for one who is growing old. No, no—banish the *Antiquary,* banish *Leatherstocking,* and banish all the world! Let us not go about to make life duller than it is.—*Books and Libraries.*

II

In Scott's narrative poems the scenery is accessory and subordinate. It is a picturesque background to his figures, a landscape through which the action rushes like a torrent, catching a hint of colour perhaps from rock or tree, but never any image so distinct that it tempts us aside to reverie or meditation.—*Address on Wordsworth.*

GOETHE ON BYRON

With a temperament which tended to transgress all bounds, he did well in imposing upon himself a certain restraint by the observance of the three unities. Would that he had known some restraint also in regard to his morals! But this was not in his nature and proved his ruin, and one may well say that he was ruined by his unbridled passions.

He was all in the dark about himself. He obeyed his passions blindly and never knew, nor thought upon, what he was doing. Permitting himself everything, and approving nothing in others, he was his own worst foe and made all the world his enemy. He offended, at the very beginning, the most eminent literary men by his *English Bards and Scotch Reviewers,* and, in order to be tolerated at all after that, he was obliged to take a step backward. In his subsequent works, he continued his opposition and his fault-finding, sparing neither State nor Church. His reckless activity made him impossible in England, and would in time have driven him from all Europe. He felt himself hemmed in everywhere, and while indulging in boundless personal licence looked upon the whole world as his prison. He did not go to Greece of his own volition, he was driven to it after he had fallen out with all the world.

His cutting loose from all that is customary and patriotic not only caused the personal ruin of this eminent man, but his revolutionary mind and his constant emotional activity prevented the proper development of his genius. Even the best of his works suffered greatly from his incessant opposition and fault-finding, for the reader is affected by the discontent of the writer, and persistent opposition ends in negation, which in the end is a mere nothing. If I speak of what is bad as bad, nothing is gained thereby. But if I call bad what is good, much harm is done. He who would achieve something must not rail at things, but ignore what is perverse, and do what is right himself. Our aim must not be to pull down, but to build up and create something that mankind may be able to enjoy.—*Eckermann's Conversations with Goethe.*

GRILLPARZER ON BYRON
1838

It is a most remarkable phenomenon that Lord Byron, the second greatest English poet, showed so little appreciation of Shakespeare, the greatest. Tieck and similar phrase-mongers may be ready with the explanation that the lesser mind simply did not understand the greater, but since these very scribblers, while being immeasurably below Lord Byron in intellect and everything else, imagine they themselves understand Shakespeare, we have to look for another explanation of Byron's indifference to Shakespeare. And there is an explanation. It lies partly in Byron's intellectual independence, partly in the modernism of everything he wrote. All his convictions were characterised by this independence, and he absorbed nothing that did not first emanate from within him. As an Englishman he was familiar with the ancients and prized them highly, because of his first youthful impressions, and because only one who is below the intellectual level of humanity can fail to appreciate them. But there is every reason to believe that he appropriated the ancients and made them his own in the same large, human way as did the great French minds, and as the practical intellects of English public life are doing at the present day. His veneration for Pope seems to imply that he did not greatly object to the manner in which that man of many tastes dealt with Homer. We Germans pay particular attention to those features of the ancients which distinguish them from us, and in a historical sense this is certainly the better way. Other nations, however, dwell chiefly on that which the ancients have in common with us moderns. With them they become practical examples, greatly influencing higher culture; while with us they have become obstacles, in a certain sense, though their glory is all the greater if we look upon them in detachment and as isolated examples. No one since the creation of the world, with the possible exception of Shakespeare, has been less of a pedant than Lord Byron, and this leads us to his second quality, his absolute modernism.

LOWELL ON BYRON

Three men, almost contemporaneous with each other,—Wordsworth, Keats, and Byron,—were the great means of bringing back English poetry from the sandy deserts of rhetoric, and recovering for her her triple inheritance of simplicity, sensuousness, and passion. Of these, Wordsworth was the only conscious reformer, and his hostility to the existing formalism injured his earlier poems by tinging them with something of iconoclastic extravagance. He was the deepest thinker, Keats the most essentially a poet, and Byron the most keenly intellectual of the three. Keats had the broadest mind, or at least his mind was open on more sides, and he was able to understand Wordsworth and judge Byron, equally conscious, through his artistic sense, of the greatness of the one and the many littlenesses of the other, while Wordsworth was isolated in a feeling of his prophetic character, and Byron had only an uneasy and jealous instinct of contemporary merit. The poems of Wordsworth, as he was the most individual, accordingly reflect the moods of his own nature; those of Keats, from sensitiveness of organisation, the moods of his own taste and feeling; and those of Byron, who was impressible chiefly through the understanding, the intellectual and moral wants of the time in which he lived. Wordsworth has influenced most the ideas of succeeding poets; Keats, their forms; and Byron, interesting to men of imagination less for his writings than for what his writings indicate, reappears no more in poetry, but presents an ideal to youth made restless with vague desires not yet regulated by experience nor supplied with motives by the duties of life.—*Essay on Keats.*

SAINTE-BEUVE ON LORD CHESTERFIELD

The Chesterfield whom we best like to study is the man of intellect and experience who has figured in political life and taken a sufficient part in public affairs to understand all their mainsprings and to lay bare their secrets. It is he who, in his youth, was the friend of Pope and Bolingbroke, who introduced Montesquieu and Voltaire to England, who corresponded with Fontenelle and Mme. de Tencin, whom the Académie des Inscriptions elected a member, who united in himself the intellect of two nations, and who, in more than one witty essay, but more particularly in his letters to his son, shows himself to us as a moralist equally amiable and accomplished, and as one of the masters of the art of life. We study in him the La Rochefoucauld of England.

Montesquieu, after the publication of *l'Esprit des Lois,* wrote to the Abbé de Guasco, who was then in England: "Tell Lord Chesterfield that nothing has gratified me so much as his praise; but now that he is reading me for the third time I hope he will be more competent than ever to tell me what to correct and set right in my work; nothing could be more instructive to me than his remarks and his criticism." It was Chesterfield who, speaking one day to Montesquieu of the readiness of the French to engage in revolutions and of their impatience with slow reforms, summed up our whole history in the sentence: "You Frenchmen may know how to make barricades, but you will never learn how to raise barriers."

Lord Chesterfield greatly enjoyed Voltaire. He said, with reference to the *Siècle de Louis Quatorze*: "Lord Bolingbroke taught me how we ought to read history, Voltaire teaches me how it ought to be written." But, at the same time, with that practical sense which never deserts men of intellect on the other side of the Channel, he recognised Voltaire's imprudences and disapproved of them. In his old age, when he had retired from society, he wrote to a French lady: "Your good writers are my principal resource; Voltaire, above all, charms me; but there is his impiety, with which he feels bound to season all he writes. If he were wise he would suppress it, for after all no one ought to disturb the existing order of things. Let every man think as he will, or rather as he can, only let him not publish his ideas if they are such as to trouble the peace of society."

What Chesterfield said in 1768, he had already said twenty-five years previously, in writing to the younger Crébillon—a curious correspondent and confidant in the matter of morals. He was then speaking of Voltaire's tragedy of *Mahomet,* and the daring things in it: "What I cannot forgive, for it is unpardonable," wrote Chesterfield to Crébillon, "is all the trouble he goes to in order to propagate a doctrine so pernicious to society and so contrary to that religious feeling common to all countries. I doubt very much whether it is permissible for any man to denounce the worship and the belief of his own land, even if he be sincerely convinced that its religion is full of errors. He must consider the pain and disorder he is sure to cause. Still more certain am I that no one can be permitted to attack the very foundation of morals and to break the ties, already weakened, which are so necessary to hold men to their duty."

Chesterfield, in writing as he did, made no mistake as to Voltaire's great inconsistency. That inconsistency, briefly, was the following: Voltaire, who liked to speak of men as fools or children, and who could not sufficiently ridicule them, yet put loaded weapons into their hands, without troubling himself in the least about the use that they might make of them.

Lord Chesterfield himself, in the eyes of the Puritans of his own country, has been accused, I ought to say, of a breach of morality in addressing his *Letters* to his son. The severe Johnson— who was in other ways prejudiced against Chesterfield, and who felt he had a grievance against him —said, when the *Letters* were first published, that "they taught the morals of a wanton and the manners of a dancing-master." Such a judgment is altogether unjust. If Chesterfield in a certain instance lays stress upon graceful manners and on the need of making every effort to please, it is only after having dwelt on the solid parts of education, so that his pupil is less in danger of sinning on the side which makes a man "respectable" than on that which makes him agreeable. Though more than one passage in these *Letters* may seem very strange as being addressed by a father to his son, yet taken as a whole, they are pervaded by a spirit of true tenderness and wisdom. If Horace had had a son, I imagine he would not have written differently to him.—*Causeries du Lundi*, Vol. II, "Lettres du Lord Chesterfield à son Fils."

GOETHE ON SHAKESPEARE

I

The greatness of Shakespeare has been acknowledged more fully by the Germans than by any other nation, perhaps even more than by his own. We have treated him with all the justice, fairness and indulgence which we deny our own kin. Our eminent writers have been busy showing us his merits in the most favourable light, and I have always readily subscribed to what has been said in his praise and honour, or even exculpation. I have on a previous occasion spoken of the influence of this extraordinary mind upon me, and what I attempted to say about his works has met with some approval. In this place I shall merely say that I am tempted to add a few further remarks as to his transcendent merits, for the benefit of such friends as may be inclined to listen to me.

For the present I shall only explain more fully how I became acquainted with him. This happened rather early in my life, at Leipsic, through Dodd's *Beauties of Shakespeare*. Whatever may be said against such collections, which present to us an author in fragments, they are not without their effect. We are not always sufficiently capable and wide-awake to take in an entire work according to its value. Are we not in the habit of marking in a book the passages that have a direct reference to ourselves? Young people especially, who have not yet acquired a thorough education, are, as is meet, attracted by brilliant passages, and I remember as one of the most beautiful periods of my life the time when that work impressed me so that I marked what most interested me. Its superb characteristics, the noble sayings, the admirable descriptions, the humorous traits —each single thing impressed me powerfully.

At this time appeared Wieland's translation. It was devoured and talked about and recommended to friends and acquaintances. We Germans have had the advantage that several important foreign works became first known to us in a pleasant and easily intelligible form. The prose translations of Shakespeare, first by Wieland, then by Eschenburg, suited as they were to the comprehension of the general reader, gained rapidly a wide circulation and produced a great impression. All honour to rhythm and rhyme, which give to poetry its peculiar charm, but what really stirs and profoundly affects us, what is truly enlightening and educating, is that which remains of the poet after his poetry has been translated into prose. Then we have the pure and perfect essence, which, if absent, a dazzling form often simulates, and, if present, conceals. I therefore consider prose translations in the early stages of youthful education of greater advantage than those in verse, for we often see that boys, who are so apt to turn everything into jest, find pleasure in the mere sound of words and the syllabic rhythm, and thus lose in a sort of parodistic perverseness, the deeper meaning of the noblest works. I would raise the question whether it may not be desirable to undertake a German prose translation of Homer, provided it can equal the best literary efforts of the day. This suggestion and what I have said before I leave to the consideration of our worthy pedagogues, who have abundant experience in such matters. But I may, in support of my remarks, call attention to Luther's translation of the Bible, for the fact that this excellent man has enriched our mother tongue by a work which, originally composed in the most diverse styles, appears to us, in its poetic, historic, hortatory and didactic aspect, as though cast in one mould—this fact has done more for the spread of religion than would have been possible if he had tried to imitate in detail all the peculiarities of the original. In vain has been the subsequent effort to render the Book of Job, the Psalms and other lyric parts of the Bible enjoyable in a poetic form. If we would influence the masses, a simple translation is always the best. Those critical translations that vie with the original serve in reality only to amuse the learned.— *Autobiography,* Part III, Book XI.

II

I do not remember that any book, any human being, any event in my life ever affected me to the same extent as those priceless plays which I learned to know through your kindness. They seem to me to be the work of some divine genius that has descended upon earth, in order to make men by gentle teachings acquainted with themselves. They are not poetic works. As one reads them one seems to stand before the colossal, open books of fate, through which storm all the passions of life, agitating the pages to and fro. The strength and tenderness, the violence and repose of these works have so astounded and overpowered me that I have the greatest longing for the hour when I shall be able to read on.—*Wilhelm Meister's Apprenticeship,* Book III, Chapter XI.

GRILLPARZER ON SHAKESPEARE
1817

One of the most admirable traits in Shakespeare's *Macbeth,* the one which, as far as I know, has been least noticed, is the attitude of·Macbeth, so diametrically opposed to that of his wife, in the resolve to do the deed and then in the deed itself.   Shakespeare has in this not only described Macbeth and his wife, but man and woman in general.   In Lady Macbeth's soul the resolve matured at its very inception.   She is the woman that acts in accordance with her feelings, whether for good or evil.   Macbeth struggles long against the idea, although (justly enough) all the arguments he uses flow not so much from the virtue of the man as from the honour of the soldier.   Lady Macbeth determines him to do the deed.   But now, when the deed is about to be performed, their relations are changed.   Macbeth shudders, but he acts; his wife, the inhuman temptress, had been before him in Duncan's room; she had the dagger in her hand—"had he not resembled my father as he slept, I had done it!"—I am often angry at myself for not giving up the idea of ever writing anything, after reading such a scene. . . .

What a happy and horrible trait, that Macbeth conceals from his wife the already planned murder

FRANZ GRILLPARZER

of Banquo, and still asks her to treat him with consideration at the banquet, although he knows well that Banquo can never come to it! Macbeth is perhaps Shakespeare's greatest work, that it is the truest admits of no doubt.

1817

Much has been said about the gift of great poets to depict the most diverse passions and characters foreign to their own nature, and there has been much talk about observing and studying man, and of how Shakespeare gathered material for his Macbeths and Othellos in taverns and among sailors and cart drivers, and how, when he had a bushelful of such impressions, he sat down and made a play of it. O the wiseacres! Genius, in my opinion, can give nothing but what it finds within itself, and will never depict any passion or conviction that it does not harbour within its own bosom. Hence it happens that some young man will look with searching eyes deep into the human heart, while one who has long been familiar with the world and its ways, sharp observer though he may be, will give you nothing but a patchwork of phrases that have been used a hundred times over and over again. Would you then say that Shakespeare must have been a murderer, thief, liar, traitor, ingrate, madman, because he has de-

picted all these in so masterly a manner? Yes!
That is to say, there must have been a tendency
to all this within him, although the predominance
of reason and the moral sense did not allow it to
come to the surface.*

1819

Much as has been said about the underlying
idea of Hamlet, I am not satisfied with any of the
explanations. It may be that the incredible and
inexplicable potency of the play lies partly in the
fact that the thread which leads through the laby-
rinth is invisible to us. Therein it resembles so
closely the momentous events of this world, and
therefore it affects us as powerfully as these do.
A ghost appears and calls for revenge; he disappears as he came, seemingly without reason;
the persons of the play are scattered to all parts
of the compass; horrible things happen, apparently to no purpose; our eyes are scarcely able
to discern the aim of it all; and just when the
tangle is greatest, irresistible fate does its work,
bringing ruin to all. Shakespeare's apparent
lack of method was clearly the result of his proceeding, step by step, to develop his melancholy
plot. The instinct of his genius furnished that
stupendous, even if loose, connection that is incomparably more effective than the ideas which

in modern plays so obtrusively impede the action, strutting visibly before us like ghosts in broad daylight.   But let no one dare to imitate Shakespeare.

1819

An English art critic has given us the seeming paradox that Falstaff was no coward.   Rightly considered, he was not.   In his youth he certainly was courageous, just as, besides his mother-wit, he had some other good qualities; but his enjoyment of life swallowed up everything else. Ease and sensual pleasure had surrounded him, as it were, with a moral tissue of fat, which grew with the physical tissue; his melancholy humour, of which he often speaks, is nothing but a semi-conscious sense of his perversity.   This largely accounts for the fact that Falstaff, let him do what he likes, never offends us, and remains our favourite to such a degree that the conclusion of the second part of Henry IV almost fails to satisfy us.   It is, however, certain that after the first half of this last play something of Shakespeare's original inspiration seems to have left him.   Everything is excellent even here, but Shakespeare could have done still better.

1823

How little particular Shakespeare's public was is shown by *The Two Gentlemen of Verona.*

What precipitation, what improbabilities are crowded into the fifth act! It is all nothing but pastime, without a human basis and without sentiment.

One must really make a good deal of allowance for the fashion of that time not to find the flowery speeches in the first act of *Romeo and Juliet* most insipid. That the change in the passion of Romeo is much too rapid and really undramatic no sensible person will deny. Shakespeare himself seems to have felt this, and to have introduced just in this passage, and nowhere else in the entire play, the chorus, contrary to all harmony. It is, however, possible that the preceding dance may have lasted pretty long, giving rise to mute and changing approaches, or that Romeo even may have danced with Juliet, to which possibly referred the words of Juliet: "A rhyme I learn'd even now of one I danc'd withal." Every such delay, every approach, every touch, softens the harshness of the situation, although precipitancy in the change of emotions (however just in itself) is one of Shakespeare's principal faults.

1823

The Tempest—The scene where Miranda falls asleep, while listening to her father's story, re-

minds one very much of a similar situation in
the *Tres Diamantes* of Lope de Vega, except that
the scene in the Spanish play is incomparably
more beautiful and at the same time forms part
of the plot; Miranda falls asleep, we do not know
why, and her sleep has no bearing on what happens afterwards. The thought has often occurred
to me, whether Shakespeare had not had vague
traditions of the Spanish drama.

1824

In his strictly historical plays Shakespeare hur-
ries rapidly over the most important moments,
over resolves and mental changes. Since these,
as historical facts, justify themselves, and were
known to the spectators, he did not stop long
enough to furnish a plausible motive, as, for instance, in the going over of Burgundy to the
French in Part I of Henry VI. This is certainly
a fault, but it is one from which one can hardly
escape in historical drama, where events crowd
themselves within a small compass. But is that
first part really by Shakespeare? Why not? It
is perhaps one of his first works, and his talent
may have been unequal to cope with the dramatic
material. In the conversation between Suffolk
and Margaret we find enough of Shakespeare.

1837

We speak of Voltaire's disparaging remarks about Shakespeare. He was, however, quite conscious of Shakespeare's merits, and indulged his ill humour only when a French author permitted himself to place Shakespeare above Racine. In the article on Intolerance (*Dictionnaire Philosophique*) he ranks him with the great minds to whom intolerance was foreign, with a Newton, Frederick the Great, Locke and Leibnitz. And these men meant much to Voltaire.

1841

Yesterday Holtei read Shakespeare's *Julius Cæsar*. We may look at it as we will, it is not a good play. The first three acts are perfectly dramatic, but after that the plot ends abruptly and the interest is purely historical. In the conversation between Brutus and Cassius, in the fourth act, there is a suggestion that Brutus acted merely for the sake of the cause, while the others were impelled by selfishness and envy. If this contrast had been adhered to and developed there might have been a complete whole; but the play runs on without further allusion to it and it ends merely as an incident, instead of being an organic whole.

1842

So much has been written about *Hamlet*. The solution of the problem lies in the melancholy which seizes upon one who is prevented from action by just doubts. When finally the inevitable moment arrives, when he must act, his nature, whose very foundation had been undermined collapses, and we have in his place Fortinbras, who acts rapidly and daringly. We must not assume that Shakespeare had thought of all this, for the true poet indulges in no such abstract reasoning while creating his works; nevertheless this was the foundation of the play, and it may be accepted by those who need an explanation beyond the impression made upon their hearts.

1843

I have often wondered whether Shakespeare, even if he did not know Spanish himself, had not some access, perhaps through a friend who knew the language, to Spanish dramatic literature. What suggested itself in reading Lope de Vega has again come to my mind in reading Lope de Rueda's *comedia de los engaños*—"Comedy of Errors."

1849

What is most characteristic of Shakespeare's intellect, and what distinguishes him from all other poets, is that the receptive or reproductive side of his nature by far outweighs the productive, or, to speak more colloquially, that the actor in him is as active as the poet. The productive imagination is busy with the creation of characters, and is satisfied with a superficial effect; but the receptive nature is emotional and penetrates into the depths of things. Imagination of this kind elaborates single details and constantly adds to the whole. It is true enough that in the poet ought to be united both receptivity and productivity, but the actor in Shakespeare was compelled to identify himself with the persons and situations, and he wrote from the standpoint of the actor, instead of creating, as a poet, images and characters which the actor might use. He lived in his characters as he wrote his plays, and he was as much the interpreter of the persons as he was their creator. For the source of his dramas he went to history or to a story, often enough even to a previous play, from the plot of which he scarcely deviated, and which he merely rounded out and enriched. How little of a poet, in the ordinary sense of the word, he was is shown by his first lyric or epic attempts, which are complete failures. *Venus and Adonis,* with all its scattered beauties, repels us by its awkward dulness, *The Rape of Lucrece* is wholly artificial. Only when Shakespeare the manager began to adapt plays for his theatre his real genius unconsciously overmastered him, and he became the greatest poet of modern times, while he himself imagined he was merely writing for his bread.

1849

The Germans consider Shakespeare a perfect image of nature. In placing him, and justly, above all poets of modern time, they are thinking mainly of the truth of his creations. Now it is remarkable that his truth to nature has not been always and everywhere acknowledged. Voltaire, as gifted a man as the world has ever seen, and moreover, in some of his dramas, no mean poet, has spoken rather disparagingly of Shakespeare, and if we consider him, not unjustly, as prejudiced, the second greatest poet of England, Lord Byron, who was himself by no means lacking in a sense of truth to nature, was far from being impressed with the transcendent merits of his great countryman. Whence comes this disparity of judgment in a matter which ought to be so firmly established for all time as nature and truth? In solving this problem we shall be greatly aided by the character of Othello—that, psychologically, most faithful picture of human passion. Iago's slanders, his fragmentary hints, Othello's struggle between passion and suspicion—all this could not be truer to nature. Thus is passion born, thus it grows, thus it finally culminates in all its fury—but all this is not in so short a time. Shakespeare gives us often a compendium, a *précis*, an *abrégé* of nature, instead of nature herself. That for which five acts would scarcely have sufficed is here compressed within the space of a single one. In the third, Othello has dismissed his lieutenant, more in the interest of military punctiliousness than because he bears him a grudge. He meets him, not in secret, but without any suspicious appearances, together with his wife, whose intercession Cassio bespeaks. She actually pleads for him. What can be more simple, natural and innocent? And yet is it possible that Othello's suspicion, within the space of a single act, can rise to such a height that the rest of the play can scarcely add anything further to it than the murder? I pass over the story of the handkerchief, which will not bear serious examination; that Desdemona uses so valuable and significant a pledge of love for an ordinary handkerchief can hardly be considered natural. Shakespeare always walks the path of nature, but he often makes short cuts. In this lies both the truth and untruth of his poetry.

1855

Shakespeare may possibly have fared like

Petrarch, who expected his posthumous fame to rest on his Latin poems, and therefore attached less importance to his sonnets, whereas posterity has forgotten the former, and remembers and admires only the sonnets. It is equally possible that Shakespeare preferred his epic and lyric poems to his dramatic works, inasmuch as the former appealed to the educated, whereas in his dramas he had to consult the taste of a public consisting, in part at least, of the uneducated. The passage in Hamlet where a most bombastic tirade from a tragedy is quoted as a perfect model of its kind, seems to point in the direction indicated. Did he perhaps think, like Lope de Vega, that it was wise to disregard dramatic rules in order to please the spectators, and was he dissatisfied with having created original masterpieces, instead of pale copies of the tragedies of Seneca? This is not to imply that Shakespeare was blind to his own merits. Whoever has produced something excellent knows that he has done it just about right, and it is possible that Shakespeare, as actor and manager, was only looking for his bread and thinking of the pleasure of the public, while delving into the depths of human nature, which, to his penetrating intellect, were nothing but surfaces. That he almost invariably only adapted or recast the plays of others may have its share in confusing the opinions of his contemporaries, who were so far mistaken as, immediately after his death, to place him below Beaumont and Fletcher. What confirms me most in my view is a subtle mannerism, something cold and affected, in his lyric and epic poems, where he was free to follow only his ideals of beauty and art.

LOWELL ON SHAKESPEARE

I

Lichtenberg says somewhere, that it was the advantage of the ancients to write before the great art of writing ill had been invented; and Shakespeare may be said to have had the good luck of coming after Spenser (to whom the debt of English poetry is incalculable) had reinvented the art of writing well. But Shakespeare arrived at a mastery in this respect which sets him above all other poets. He is not only superior in degree, but he is also different in kind. In that less purely artistic sphere of style which concerns the matter rather than the form, his charm is often unspeakable. How perfect his style is may be judged from the fact that it never curdles into mannerism, and thus absolutely eludes imitation. Though here, if anywhere, the style is the man, yet it is noticeable only, like the images of Brutus, by its absence, so thoroughly is he absorbed in his work, while he fuses thought and word indissolubly together, till all the particles cohere by the best virtue of each. With perfect truth he has said of himself that he writes:

> "All one, ever the same,
> Putting invention in a noted weed,
> That every word doth almost tell his name."

And yet who has so succeeded in imitating him as to remind us of him by even so much as the gait of a single verse? Those magnificent crystallisations of feeling and phrase, basaltic masses, molten and interfused by the primal fires of passion, are not to be reproduced by the slow experiments of the laboratory striving to parody creation with artifice. Mr. Matthew Arnold seems to think that Shakespeare has damaged English poetry. I wish he had! It is true he lifted Dryden above himself in "All for Love"; but it was Dryden who said of him, by instinctive conviction rather than judgment, that within his magic circle none dared tread but he. Is he to blame for the extravagances of modern diction, which are but the reaction of the brazen age against the degeneracy of art into artifice, that has characterised the silver period in every literature? We see in them only the futile effort of misguided persons to torture out of language the secret of that inspiration which should be in themselves. We do not find the extravagances in Shakespeare himself. I never saw a line in any modern poet that reminded me of him, and will venture to assert that it is only poets of the second class that find successful imitators. And the reason seems to me a very plain one. The genius of the great poet seeks repose in the expression of itself, and finds it at last in style, which is the establishment of a perfect mutual understanding between the worker and his material. The secondary intellect, on the other hand, seeks for excitement in expression, and stimulates itself into mannerism, which is the wilful obtrusion of self, as style is its unconscious abnegation. No poet of the first class has ever left a school, because his imagination is incommunicable; while, just as surely as the thermometer tells of the neighbourhood of an iceberg, you may detect the presence of a genius of the second class in any generation by the influence of his mannerism, for that, being an artificial thing, is capable of reproduction. Dante, Shakespeare, Goethe, left no heirs either to the form or mode of their expression; while Milton, Sterne, and Wordsworth left behind them whole regiments uniformed with all their external characteristics.

I do not mean that great poetic geniuses may not have influenced thought (though I think it would be difficult to show how Shakespeare had done so, directly and wilfully), but that they have not infected contemporaries or followers with mannerism. The quality in him which makes him at once so thoroughly English and so thoroughly cosmopolitan is that aëration of the understanding by the imagination which he has in common with all the greater poets, and which is the privilege of genius. The modern school, which mistakes violence for intensity, seems to catch its breath when it finds itself on the verge of natural expression, and to say to itself, "Good heavens! I had almost forgotten I was inspired!" But of Shakespeare we do not even suspect that he ever remembered it. He does not always speak in that intense way that flames up in *Lear* and *Macbeth* through the rifts of a soil volcanic with passion. He allows us here and there the repose of a commonplace character, the consoling distraction of a humorous one. He knows how to be equable and grand without effort, so that we forget the altitude of thought to which he has led us, because the slowly receding slope of a mountain stretching downward by ample gradations gives a less startling impression of height than to look over the edge of a ravine that makes but a wrinkle in its flank.

II

The hold which Shakespeare has acquired and maintained upon minds so many and so various, in so many vital respects utterly unsympathetic and even incapable of sympathy with his own, is one of the most noteworthy phenomena in the history of literature. That he has had the most inadequate of editors, that, as his own Falstaff was the cause of the wit, so he has been the cause of the foolishness that was in other men (as where Malone ventured to discourse upon his metres, and Dr. Johnson on his imagination), must be apparent to every one,—and also that his genius and its manifestations are so various, that there is no commentator but has been able to illustrate him from his own peculiar point of view or from the results of his own favourite studies. But to show that he was a good common lawyer, that he understood the theory of colours, that he was an accurate botanist, a master of the science of medicine, especially in its relation to mental disease, a profound metaphysician, and of great experience and insight in politics,—all these, while they may very well form the staple of separate treatises, and prove, that, whatever the extent of his learning, the range and accuracy of his knowledge were beyond precedent or later parallel, are really outside the province of an editor.

III

We admire in Homer the blind placid mirror of
the world's young manhood, the bard who escapes
from his misfortune in poems all memory, all life
and bustle, adventure and picture; we revere in
Dante that compressed force of life-long passion
which could make a private experience cosmopolitan in its reach and everlasting in its significance; we respect in Goethe the Aristotelian poet,
wise by weariless observation, witty with intention, the stately *Geheimrath* of a provincial court
in the empire of Nature. As we study these, we
seem in our limited way to penetrate into their
consciousness and to measure and master their
methods; but with Shakespeare it is just the other
way; the more we have familiarised ourselves with
the operations of our own consciousness, the more
do we find, in reading him, that he has been before-
hand with us, and that, while we have been vainly
endeavouring to find the door of his being, he has
searched every nook and cranny of our own.
While other poets and dramatists embody isolated
phases of character, and work inward from the
phenomenon to the special law which it illustrates,
he seems in some strange way unitary with human
nature itself, and his own soul to have been the
law and life-giving power of which his creations
are only the phenomena. We justify or criticise

the characters of other writers by our memory and experience, and pronounce them natural or unnatural; but he seems to have worked in the very stuff of which memory and experience are made, and we recognise his truth to Nature by an innate and unacquired sympathy, as if he alone possessed the secret of the "ideal form and universal mould," and embodied generic types rather than individuals. In this Cervantes alone has approached him; and Don Quixote and Sancho, like the men and women of Shakespeare, are the contemporaries of every generation, because they are not products of an artificial and transitory society, but because they are animated by the primeval and unchanging forces of that humanity which underlies and survives the forever-fickle creeds and ceremonials of the parochial corners which we who dwell in them sublimely call The World.

IV

The Attic tragedy still keeps its hold upon the loyalty of scholars through their imagination, or their pedantry, or their feeling of an exclusive property, as may happen, and, however alloyed with baser matter, this loyalty is legitimate and well bestowed. But the dominion of the Shakespearian is even wider. It pushes forward its boundaries from year to year, and moves no land-

mark backward. Here Alfieri and Lessing own a
common allegiance; and the loyalty to him is one
not of guild or tradition, but of conviction and
enthusiasm. Can this be said of any other modern? of robust Corneille? of tender Racine? of
Calderon even, with his tropical warmth and
vigour of production? The Greeks and he are
alike and alone in this, and for the same reason,
that both are unapproachably the highest in their
kind. Call him Gothic, if you like, but the inspiring mind that presided over the growth of
these clustered masses of arch and spire and pinnacle and buttress is neither Greek nor Gothic,—
it is simply genius lending itself to embody the
new desire of man's mind, as it had embodied the
old. After all, to be delightful is to be classic,
and the chaotic never pleases long. But manifold-
ness is not confusion, any more than formalism is
simplicity. If Shakespeare rejected the unities,
as I think he who complains of "Art made tongue-
tied by Authority" might very well deliberately
do, it was for the sake of an imaginative unity
more intimate than any of time and place. The
antique in itself is not the ideal, though its re-
moteness from the vulgarity of every-day associa-
tions helps to make it seem so. The true ideal is
not opposed to the real, nor is it any artificial
heightening thereof, but lies *in* it, and blessed are

the eyes that find it! It is the *mens divinior* which hides within the actual, transfiguring matter-of-fact into matter-of-meaning for him who has the gift of second-sight. In this sense Hogarth is often more truly ideal than Raphael, Shakespeare often more truly so than the Greeks. I think it is a more or less conscious perception of this ideality, as it is a more or less well-grounded persuasion of it as respects the Greeks, that assures to him, as to them, and with equal justice, a permanent supremacy over the minds of men. This gives to his characters their universality, to his thought its irradiating property, while the artistic purpose running through and combining the endless variety of scene and character will alone account for his power of dramatic effect. Goethe affirmed, that, without Schröder's prunings and adaptations, Shakespeare was too undramatic for the German theatre,—that, if the theory that his plays should be represented textually should prevail, he would be driven from the boards. The theory has prevailed, and he not only holds his own, but is acted oftener than ever. It is not irregular genius that can do this, for surely Germany need not go abroad for what her own Werners could more than amply supply her with.

But I would much rather quote a fine saying than a bad prophecy of a man to whom I owe so

much. Goethe, in one of the most perfect of his
shorter poems, tells us that a poem is like a painted
window. Seen from without (and he accordingly
justifies the Philistine, who never looks at them
otherwise), they seem dingy and confused enough;
but enter, and then

> "Da ist's auf einmal farbig helle,
>   Geschicht' und Zierath glänzt in Schnelle."

With the same feeling he says elsewhere in
prose, that "there is a destructive criticism and a
productive. The former is very easy; for one has
only to set up in his mind any standard, any model,
however narrow" (let us say the Greeks), "and
then boldly assert that the work under review
does not match with it, and therefore is good for
nothing,—the matter is settled, and one must at
once deny its claim. Productive criticism is a
great deal more difficult; it asks, What did the
author propose to himself? Is what he proposes
reasonable and comprehensible? and how far has
he succeeded in carrying it out?" It is in applying this latter kind of criticism to Shakespeare
that the Germans have set us an example worthy
of all commendation. If they have been sometimes over-subtile, they at least had the merit of
first looking at his works as wholes, as something
that very likely contained an idea, perhaps con-

veyed a moral, if we could get at it. The illu-
mination lent us by most of the English commentators reminds us of the candles which guides
hold up to show us a picture in a dark place, the
smoke of which gradually makes the work of the
artist invisible under its repeated layers. Lessing, as might have been expected, opened the first
glimpse in the new direction; Goethe followed with
his famous exposition of Hamlet; A. W. Schlegel
took a more comprehensive view in his Lectures,
which Coleridge worked over into English, adding many fine criticisms of his own on single passages; and finally, Gervinus has devoted four volumes to a comment on the plays, full of excellent
matter, though pushing the moral exegesis beyond
all reasonable bounds. With the help of all these,
and especially of the last, I shall apply this theory
of criticism to Hamlet, not in the hope of saying
anything new, but of bringing something to the
support of the thesis, that, if Shakespeare was
skilful as a playwright, he was even greater as
a dramatist,—that if his immediate business was
to fill the theatre, his higher object was to create
something which, by fulfilling the conditions and
answering the requirements of modern life, should
as truly deserve to be called a work of art as
others had deserved it by doing the same thing
in former times and under other circumstances.

Supposing him to have accepted—consciously or not is of little importance—the new terms of the problem which makes character the pivot of dramatic action, and consequently the key of dramatic unity, how far did he succeed?—*Shakespeare Once More.*

———————

Webster was a far more considerable man than Marston, and infinitely above him in genius. Without the poetic nature of Marlowe, or Chapman's somewhat unwieldy vigour of thought, he had that inflammability of mind which, untempered by a solid understanding, made his plays a strange mixture of vivid expression, incoherent declamation, dramatic intensity, and extravagant conception of character.   He was not, in the highest sense of the word, a great dramatist.   Shakespeare is the only one of that age.   Marlowe had a rare imagination, a delicacy of sense that made him the teacher of Shakespeare and Milton in versification, and was, perhaps, as purely a poet as any that England has produced; but his mind had no balance-wheel.   Chapman abounds in splendid enthusiasms of diction, and now and then dilates our imaginations with suggestions of profound poetic depth.   Ben Jonson was a conscientious and intelligent workman, whose plays glow, here and there, with the golden pollen of that poetic feeling with which his age impregnated all thought and expression; but his leading characteristic, like that of his great namesake, Samuel, was a hearty common sense, which fitted him rather to be a great critic than a great poet. He had a keen and ready eye for the comic in situation, but no humour. Fletcher was as much a poet as fancy and sentiment can make any man. Only Shakespeare wrote comedy and tragedy with truly ideal elevation and breadth. Only Shakespeare had that true sense of humour which, like the universal solvent sought by the alchemists, so fuses together all the elements of a character (as in Falstaff), that any question of good or evil, of dignified or ridiculous, is silenced by the apprehension of its thorough humanity. Rabelais shows gleams of it in Panurge; but, in our opinion, no man ever possessed it in an equal degree with Shakespeare, except Cervantes; no man has since shown anything like an approach to it (for Molière's quality was comic power rather than humour), except Sterne, Fielding, and perhaps Richter. Only Shakespeare was endowed with that healthy equilibrium of nature whose point of rest was midway between the imagination and the understanding,—that perfectly unruffled brain which reflected all objects with almost inhuman impartiality,—that outlook whose range was ecliptical, dominating all zones of human thought and action,—that power of veri-similar conception which could take away Richard III from History, and Ulysses from Homer,—and that creative faculty whose equal touch is alike vivifying in Shallow and in Lear.—*Library of Old Authors.*

FRENCH LITERATURE

GOETHE ON VOLTAIRE

SINCE the sixteenth century the course of French literature had never been completely interrupted, political and religious disturbances within and wars without had merely quickened its progress; but the universal opinion was that already a hundred years ago it had been in full bloom. Favouring circumstances had enabled the nation to reap on all sides a rich literary harvest, and the greatest talents of the eighteenth century had to be content with a modest aftermath. Nevertheless, much had since become antiquated: comedy first of all, which was ever in need of fresh blood in order to be, even if less perfect, in accord with present life and custom, and to awaken new interest. Many tragedies had disappeared from the stage, and Voltaire was not slow in seizing the favourable opportunity of editing the works of Corneille, in order to show up the defects of his predecessor, whom, according to the general verdict, he had never equalled.

This very Voltaire, however, the marvel of his time, had himself grown old, as old as the litera-

ture of which for nearly a century he had been
the vivifying and ruling spirit. Beside him there
still existed or vegetated, in a more or less active
and happy old age, many literary dilettantes, who
gradually, one by one, disappeared. Social influences upon authors became more and more
marked, for the best society, composed of persons
of noble birth, high rank and great fortune, chose
literature as one of its favourite pastimes, thereby rendering it fashionable, and elevating it in
turn. Persons of high station and literary men
thus mutually cultivated and of necessity per-
verted one another, for gentility is exclusive,
and French criticism became exclusive, carp-
ing, fault-finding and defamatory. Thus did the
upper classes judge the writers; thus, with less
self-restraint, judged the writers each other and
even their patrons. If the public could not be
awed, it might at least be startled, or persuaded by
a show of humility, and apart from the internal
commotions of Church and State, there resulted
from all this such a literary unrest that Voltaire
needed the fullest use of all his energy and
prestige to keep himself above the level of the
general depreciation. As it was, he was openly
called a wilful old child, his incessant activity was
looked upon as the busy vanity of decrepit age;
the principles of a life-time, to the spread of

which he had so assiduously devoted himself, were no longer honoured and appreciated; nay, the very deity which he still upheld, in order to meet the reproach of atheism, was not considered valid. Thus the literary patriarch himself was forced, like the youngest of his competitors, to watch the passing moment, curry favour with men of the hour, overwhelm his friends with marks of his attention and his enemies with proofs of his dislike, and while seemingly engaged in the passionate pursuit of truth, to act falsely and deceitfully. Was it worth while to have lived so great and active a life if it was to end in greater dependence than it had begun? His lofty intellect and his delicate sensibility fully realised how intolerable such a position was. He occasionally sought relief in leaps and plunges, indulged his humour to the full, and his indiscriminate sword-thrusts provoked the indignation alike of friend and foe, for every one thought he could look through his tactics, though no one could imitate them. A public which listens only to the opinions of the aged becomes easily over-wise, and nothing is more unsatisfactory than a mature judgment adopted by an immature mind.

We young men, with our German fidelity to nature and truth, who ever considered honesty towards ourselves and others as the best guide in life and knowledge, became more and more irritated by Voltaire's dishonest partisanship and his belittlement of so many worthy objects, so that we turned from him with increased dislike. There seemed to be no limit to his abuse of religion and the sacred books upon which it is founded. He could not go far enough in his warfare against priestcraft, and all this affected me at times very disagreeably. And when I finally learned that, in order to discredit the story of the deluge, he denied the existence of fossil shells and spoke of them merely as freaks of nature, I lost the last vestige of confidence in him, for my own eyes had shown me on the Baschberg plainly enough that I stood upon ancient sea-bottom among the *exuviæ* of its original inhabitants. In very truth, these mountains had once been covered by water, whether before or after the flood was indifferent to me; enough that the valley of the Rhine had been a stupendous lake, an illimitable bay, and nothing could shake this conviction. I was only bent on extending my knowledge of land and mountains, let the result be what it might.— *Autobiography,* Part III, Book XI.

GOETHE ON MADAME DE STAËL

Her appearance, both in an intellectual and physical sense, had something charming about it, and she did not seem to be displeased when people showed themselves susceptible to her attractions. Often enough she must have been swayed, at one and the same time, by sentiments of sociability, friendly interest, affection and passion. She said once: "I have never trusted any man who has not, at some time, been in love with me." The remark is a just one, for when once, as happens in love, a man has opened his heart and committed himself, he has offered that which can never be taken back, and it would be impossible for him thereafter to harm or leave unprotected the object of his former affection.

With real impetuosity she pursued her purpose of learning to know our circle, interpreting the conditions under which we lived according to her lights. She inquired as far as possible into particulars, sought, as a woman of the world, to understand clearly our social relations, and to grasp, with her feminine powers and brilliant intellect, our general ways of thinking—all that is commonly understood by the word philosophy. Although I had no reason for concealing my thoughts in talking to her—in spite of the fact that, no matter how natural I might be, people would never take me exactly as I was—there occurred a circumstance that taught me to be cautious for the time being. I had just received a recently

published French book containing the correspondence of some women with Rousseau, who had
plainly mystified that shy and inaccessible man.
Engaging his attention at first in some trifling
matters, they enticed him into exchanging letters
with them, which, after they tired of the joke, they
gathered together into a book. I expressed to
Mme. de Staël my disapproval of such an action.
She, however, took the matter lightly, and appeared rather to approve of it. Indeed, she
hinted to me pretty plainly that it was her intention to act similarly in dealing with all of us here.
This was quite sufficient to put me on my guard
and to cause me to be somewhat reserved.

The great merits of this high-minded and
deeply sensitive authoress are apparent to every
one, and the results of her travels in Germany
show how well she employed her time. Her aims
were various. She wanted to learn all about
Weimar, in its ethical, social, and literary aspects,
and to obtain the most exact information. It was
also her wish to make herself known, being as
anxious to expound her own views as to fathom
ours. Nor was this all. She wished to impress
our senses and our emotions, as well as our intelligence, and to rouse us to a certain active interest, the absence of which she deplored. Having no conception of the meaning of duty, no idea

of the reserve and self-denial which the strict performance of it imposes, she was eager to see every
one around her in constant activity, just as in a
social circle one expects general animation and
lively talk.

The people of Weimar are not incapable of enthusiasm—it may be occasionally false enthusiasm, but French flash-fire was not to be expected
of them; least of all at a time when the whole
world was threatened by French preponderance,
and sane and quiet observers foresaw the inevitable calamities which in the following year were
to bring us to the verge of ruin. Mme. de Staël
was equally anxious to win laurels as a reader
and reciter. A reading of *Phèdre,* however, had
the success that was to be expected. It showed
once more that Germans have for ever emanci-
pated themselves from so narrow a form, so
measured and hollow a pathos. They would
rather do without the hidden core, pleasing and
natural as that is, than laboriously pick it out
from among all the unnaturalness that hides
it.

What is called philosophising in company is
merely a lively discussion concerning insoluble
problems. Of this she was passionately fond.
She carried debates on such subjects to the point
of introducing thoughts and sentiments which

ought to be reserved by each individual for communion with his Maker. . . .

Whatever one may think or say of such matters, it must be admitted that she exercised an important and lasting influence. The work on Germany, which owes its origin to the social meetings described, must be regarded as an important agency in abolishing those ancient prejudices which, like a Chinese wall, separated us from France. It was owing to her that people across the Rhine and, later, across the Channel, finally became better acquainted with us, and that we were thence able to influence vitally those Western nations. We may therefore bless that conflict between national peculiarities which for the time being seemed such an annoying obstacle to profitable intercourse.— *Annals,* 1804.

GRILLPARZER ON MADAME DE STAËL
1816

There is a peculiar atmosphere of sultriness hovering over the first volumes of Mme. de Staël's *Corinne.* It was a real relief to me when I read to-day in the second part the passage where Lord Nelvil rides across the Bridge of the Angels. I experienced a peculiar sensation, partly of joy and partly of astonishment, on finding that one of the heroes of the book could actually ride horse-

back, that is to say, was able to do something besides *talk*. I have not yet wholly finished the
book, but the plan seems to me one of the queerest
ever conceived. Variety may be pleasant enough
in itself, but not so with abrupt changes between
warm sentiment and cold reason, unless humour
unites the two extremes. Without humour, and
this is the case in *Corinne,* sentiment loses its
warmth, and reason its coolness.

1816

It is interesting to draw a parallel between Jean
Paul's *Titan* and Mme. de Staël's *Corinne.* Both
seem to have proceeded from the same plan (Jean
Paul, of course, only in the beginning of his work),
both seek to heighten the interest in Italy by describing the landscape while treating of the characters, but how different is the result! While the
landscape remains a mere background with Jean
Paul, it swallows up the characters in *Corinne.*

1822

The ridiculous vanity of Mme. de Staël is nowhere so apparent as in her last work: *Ten Years
of My Exile.* Altogether I find the ways of this
woman intolerable. What exaggerated declama-
tions! What enthusiasms, forced, if not fabri-
cated, what half-true truths and sweeping general-

isations, which, at the utmost, can only in excep-
tional cases hold water. In what did her misfortune in exile exist? In the fact that she could no
longer shine in those Paris circles for which she
had so silly an attachment. Her lamentations
are a crime against all those who at that time had
real cause for complaint.

GOETHE ON MOLIÈRE

I

I have known and loved Molière from my youth,
and have during my life learned much from him.
I read some of his plays every year, in order to
keep before me what is so truly admirable. It is
not merely the perfection of his artistic treatment
that delights me, but also his amiability and great
intellectual refinement. Molière has a grace and a
feeling for what is proper and required in good
society which, with all the innate beauty of his
nature, he could only acquire by daily intercourse
with the most eminent men of his age. I know
only the few fragments of Menander, but these
give me an equally high idea of him, and I consider this great Greek as the only man worthy to
be compared with Molière. . . .

To a man like Schlegel so genuine a nature as
Molière's is a veritable eyesore; he feels that he

has not a particle of Molière's genius in his veins, and therefore cannot tolerate him. The *Misanthrope,* which is one of my favourite pieces, and which I read over and over again, goes against Schlegel's grain; to *Tartuffe* he is forced to give a little faint praise, and then proceeds to find fault with it as much as he can. Schlegel cannot forgive Molière for ridiculing the affectations of learned women; he probably feels, as one of my friends has remarked, that had he lived in the days of Molière he himself would have been the butt of the poet's ridicule.

It cannot be denied that Schlegel knows a great deal, and one is fairly appalled at his extraordinary attainments and his wide reading. But all this is not enough. Learning is one thing, judgment another. His criticism is all one-sided. He looks in all plays merely for the skeleton of the plot and its orderly arrangement, and contents himself with pointing out little resemblances with the great plays of the past, without caring in the least for that graceful animation and evidence of high culture on the part of the author which the play may furnish. But of what use are all the artifices of talent if a dramatic piece does not reflect the amiable characteristics or the great personality of the author?—*Eckermann's Conversations with Goethe.*

II

Molière is so great that one is astonished anew
every time one reads him.   He is a man apart—
his plays border on the tragic, they take hold of
one (*sie sind apprehensiv*), and no one dares to
imitate him.   His *Miser,* where vices counteract
all the natural respect between father and son, is
particularly great, and tragic in the highest sense.
But when, as was done in a German adaptation,
the son is changed into a relative, the play is en-
feebled and loses its significance.   This was done
from fear of making vice appear in its true nature, but what becomes of it then, and is it not
precisely the insupportable that is always effective
in   tragedy?—*Eckermann's   Conversations   with
Goethe.*

GRILLPARZER ON MOLIÈRE

I do not doubt for a moment that Molière por-
trayed himself in *Le Misanthrope*.   First of all,
the play teems with those intimate little touches
which only he can discover who has himself experienced what is being represented.   That the
misanthrope's opinion of poetry was Molière's
own, no one will deny.   This seems to be confirmed even by the unsatisfactory, pointless conclusion of the play—a characteristic feature of
every poetic work which is the result of self-irony,

as witness Goethe's *Wilhelm Meister* and *Tasso*. How Molière was tortured by jealousy—well-founded jealousy, indeed—is shown by the story of his life.   And how sad was this life as a whole! We see a poet, in the real sense of the word, who is intent upon what is great and noble, and who yet is frightened off by repeated failure from the representation of serious characters upon the stage, and is forced to play the merry-andrew and clown, in all probability despising himself, in the midst of all the applause of the multitude, for sinning against his own better self.   In society, his position was far below those whom he could not look upon as his equals.   Even the *Misanthrope* was a failure, as not being farcical enough.   Was not the natural result a hostile attitude toward social conditions?   I am impelled to think of Raimund, who, while occupying a far lower rank than Molière, yet bears in this respect some resemblance to him.   How closely Molière was drawn toward emotional poetry—from which indeed he was kept back only by the spirit of the age, and perhaps by the commanding influence of his friend Boileau—is shown by various passages throughout his works, and particularly by the little fragment *Mélicerte*.   The monologue of the heroine in the second act testifies to a depth of sentiment far in advance of his time and rare even in Racine.*

SAINTE-BEUVE ON MOLIÈRE

In poetry and literature there is a class of men who have not their equal, even among the very first; not a numerous class—perhaps not more than five or six, counting from the very beginning —who have the character of universality and of an eternal humanity combined with an intimate picture of the morals and passions of their time. Facile geniuses, strong and productive, their principal traits are found in that mixture of fertility, firmness and frankness which springs from opulent knowledge and genuine indifference to conventional ways and styles. Every frame suits their picture, any point of departure is the right one for entering upon their subject; theirs is a constantly active art, which triumphs over every obstacle; it is art at its ripest, working without artifice or cumbersome apparatus.

In the Greek past, after the grand figure of Homer, with whom this class so gloriously begins, and who gives us the primitive genius of the finest part of mankind, it is not easy to know whom to name next. Sophocles, with all his seeming fecundity and with all the humanity he shows in the harmonious expression of sentiment and sorrow, stands before us so perfect in outline, so sacred, if the word be permitted, in form and attitude that we cannot tolerate the thought of taking him from his purely Greek pedestal. The famous comedians are wholly lacking; we have only the name of Menander, who was perhaps the most perfect of those geniuses we are considering; for Aristophanes's marvellous fancy, so thoroughly Athenian and so charming, makes him less universal. In Rome I can see no one but Plautus, a writer not yet sufficiently appreciated, a powerful and versatile painter of life, manager of a theatrical company, actor and author himself, like Shakespeare and Molière, whose rightful progenitor he was. But Latin literature was too obviously imported, too artificial from its very beginning, copied as it was from the Greek, to give scope to wholly unfettered genius. The most prolific of the great writers of that literature are also too distinctly "literary" and, at bottom, rhymsters—Ovid and Cicero, for instance. Nevertheless, it may claim the honour of having produced the two most admirable poets of all imitative literature, of the literature of study and taste— those chastened and perfect types, Virgil and Horace.

We must go to modern times and the Renaissance to find the men we are seeking—Shakespeare, Cervantes, Rabelais, Molière, and two or three others after them, of unequal rank. That is all; we can recognise them by their resemblances. These men had diverse and troubled destinies; they suffered, they struggled and they loved. Soldiers, physicians, comedians, and captives, they found it hard to live; they underwent the torments of misery and of passion, and were involved in all sorts of difficulties and adventures. But their genius triumphed over all obstacles, and without complaining of their fetters they shook the yoke from their necks and freed their elbows. We have all seen how natural beauty forces itself to the light in the midst of poverty, foul air and low life; we sometimes encounter those charming daughters of the poorer classes whose forms are, as it were, illumined by a mysterious perfection, whose grace extends to their very finger tips; human beings such as these keep alive the idea of the nobility of the human race as an image of the divinity. So those rare men who are endowed with genius of an exquisite and supple beauty—beauty inborn and genuine—triumph with apparent ease over the most adverse conditions, developing and asserting themselves irresistibly. Nor is their development favoured by chance and circumstance, as is that of geniuses of the second rank, such as Ovid, Dryden and the Abbé Prévost. Their work, fully as varied and prompt in appearance as that of writers of merely facile genius, is at the same time well thought out, powerful, complex on occasion, never finished until perfect and, when finished, superb. But the secret of their achievement never lies in that excessive toil, that constantly correcting thought of the studious and polished class of poets, of the Grays, Popes and Despréaux, of those poets whom I admire and enjoy as much as any one, whose scrupulous accuracy is, as I well know, one of their indispensable qualities and charms, and who seem to have taken for their motto Vauvenargues's admirable saying, "Precision is the varnish of the masters." There is in the very perfection of the great poets of the other kind something freer and bolder, an unsought irregularity incomparably more fruitful and wholly independent of ingenious fetters; a something which, springing from nowhere, playfully goes its own way, which amazes and disconcerts poets of contemporary fame by its wealth of resources, down to the minutest details of the craft. This explains why Boileau, in addition to so many other natural reasons for surprise, could not refrain from asking Molière where he found his rhymes.

Rightly understood, those great geniuses we are considering occupy a middle ground between the poesy of primitive times and that of the centuries of civilisation and culture, between the Homeric

and the Alexandrine ages.   They are the glorious,
still mighty representatives of these periods of
transition, continuing in their marked individuali-
ties the traditions of the first, while it merges into
the second.   In all things there is a first flowering,
a first and abundant harvest; these happy mortals
merely stretch out their hands and throw into the
earth, once for all, countless seeds; after them and
all around them others struggle, watch and glean.
These opulent geniuses—no longer divine and
hoary sages or mythical blind men—read, compare, imitate, like others of their day; but withal
they create as in the dawn of the ages.   Their
daily output varies in value, but among their productions we find masterpieces in which nature and
art blend in perfection.   They have grasped the
secret of art in all its extent and fulness without
thinking much about it, as others are doing; and
they practise their art day and night with a wonderful absence of self-preoccupation and literary
conceit.   Not rarely they die, as happened also in
the primitive ages, before their works are all
printed or at least properly collected and edited,
differing therein from their contemporaries, the
fashionable poets and literary lions, who look out
for these things in due time.   But such negligence
and prodigality are characteristic of those great
ones.   They rely entirely on general good sense,

on the final judgment of the people, though they know as well as the poets who pretend to despise these vulgar judgments that the people are not infallible. In a word, the great ones seem to me to be descended from the very genius of poesy as embodied in man, continuing in their persons its perpetual tradition.

Molière is one of these illustrious witnesses. Although he concerns himself chiefly with the comic side of mankind, with its contradictions, vices, deformities and eccentricities, seldom touching upon the pathetic side, and then only in passing, he yields to no one in perfection; so greatly does he excel in his own field, over which his fancy and his powerful observation roam at will, as a king in his domain,—a domain which embraces half of mankind, that half which we most frequently meet in society as it is.

Molière belongs to the age in which he lived by his pictures of certain oddities and his presentation of peculiar manners and customs, but in reality he belongs to all ages; we have in him human nature in all its phases. To take the full measure of his genius, we only have to see with what ease he grasps all that is characteristic of his century, and how completely he detaches himself from it, how closely he adapts himself to it, and with what grandeur he steps out of it. His illustrious contemporaries, Despréaux, Racine, Bossuet, Pascal, are much more distinctly men of their time, of the period of Louis XIV, than Molière. Their genius (I am speaking of the very greatest) bears the special mark of the day in which they had their being; other times would have impressed them quite differently. What would Bossuet be to-day? What would Pascal write? Racine and Boileau fit wonderfully into the reign of Louis XIV, with all its youthful brilliancy and gallantry, its victories, its intelligence. Bossuet dominates this reign at its climax, before extreme bigotry set in, though already in a period of deep religiousness. Molière, who perhaps would have been oppressed by the growing authority of religion, and who died in time to escape it— Molière, who, like Boileau and Racine (though much older than they) belonged to the earlier period, was far more independent of its tradition, although he paints it to the life as no one else did. He adds to the majestic splendour of the "grand age"; but he neither bears its mark nor suffers by its limitations; he lends his stature to it, but it cannot hold him.

The sixteenth century had, on the whole, witnessed a vast disintegration of the old religions, the Catholic and feudal order of things, and a new philosophy seized thinkers and the middle classes

of society. But the change took place in the midst
of the greatest disturbances, of a veritable orgy of
the intellect, and the bloodiest anarchy of ma-
terialism. France was, above all other countries,
the scene of this advent of a new spirit, and its
instruments were Rabelais and the League. It
was the mission of the seventeenth century to restore order, to reorganise society and religion and
encourage independence; with the reign of Henry
IV begins this task, and the age reaches its fullest
monarchical expression, with all the pomp that
crowns the attainment of so high an aim, under
Louis XIV. I shall not attempt to enumerate all
the stern efforts made, from the beginning of the
seventeenth century, to rally in the religious
centres the legions of Christ, and to reconstitute
Christian doctrine by communities, endowed con-
gregations, reformed abbeys, and this in the very
bosom of the University and of the Sorbonne.

All this is seen and reflected in literature. To
the Gallic, irreverent, mocking and indecent literature of Marot, Bonaventure, Desperiers, Rabelais,
Regnier, to the pagan literature—Greek and epi-
curean—of Ronsard, Baïf and Jodelle, to the literature of the philosophers and sceptics, Montaigne and Charron, succeeded one of a very different and opposite character. Malherbe, formal
as a man and a writer, of caustic and even cynical

mind—as Buffon was in the intervals of his noble
phrases—Malherbe, a free-thinker at heart, has
nothing Christian about his odes except the outward shell; but the genius of Corneille, the
father of *Polyeucte* and *Pauline,* is already profoundly Christian. So was that of D'Urfé. Balzac, a vain and pompous *bel esprit* and a learned
rhetorician dealing in words, is in form and idea
wedded to orthodoxy. The school of Port-
Royal was founded, and the antagonist of doubt
and of Montaigne, Pascal, appeared on the
scene. The detestable poetic school of Louis
XIII, Boisrobert, Ménage, Costar, Conrart,
d'Assoncy, Saint-Amant, etc., did not enter upon
the path of reform; that school has little seriousness and morality, it is modelled after the Italian,
a mere insipid repetition of the literature of the
Valois. But that which succeeds and smothers
it, under Louis XIV, ranges itself gradually on
the side of faith and order—witness Despréaux,
Racine, Bossuet. Even La Fontaine, with all his
bonhomie and his frailties, and wholly of the sixteenth century as he was, had his fits of religiousness when he wrote the *Captivité de Saint-Malc*
and the epistle to Mme. de La Sablière, and he
ended by repenting. In a word, the farther we
advance in the so-called age of Louis XIV, the
more we find literature, poetry, the pulpit, the

stage, in fact all the important phases of the intellect, taking on a religious and Christian character; and all the more do they betray, even in the expression of general sentiments, a return to belief in revelation and in the humanity seen *in* and *through* Jesus Christ. This is one of the profoundest and most characteristic traits of that immortal literature. The seventeenth century forms thus a solid dyke between the sixteenth and the eighteenth.

Molière, however,—I mention it without implying either praise or blame, and solely as proof of his independent genius—Molière cannot be regarded from this point of view. Although his figure and his work stand out more prominently than those of any one else within that extraordinary period of Louis the Great, he extends beyond it and reaches forward and backward, in all directions; he belongs to the region of a calmer thought, a region vaster and more universal. A pupil of Gassendi, a friend of Bernier, of Chapelle and De Hesnault, he is directly connected with the philosophy and literature of the sixteenth century; he has no antipathy toward that century or what remained of it; he did not identify himself with any reactionary movement, religious or literary, as did Bossuet, Racine and Boileau in their several ways, and as others did during three-fourths of the period of Louis XIV. He continues the line of Rabelais, Montaigne, Larivey and Regnier, of the authors of the *Satyre Ménip-pée;* he would have had no difficulty in coming to an understanding with Lamothe-le-Vayer, Naudé, or even Guy Patin, that mordant person-age, doctor of medicine though he was.

Molière belongs naturally to the world of Ninon and of Mme. de la Sablière before her con-version; he receives at Auteuil Des Barreaux and a number of young seigneurs, who were some-thing of libertines. I do not by any means wish to say that Molière was a free-thinker, either in his works or in his heart; that he had a full-fledged system upon these subjects; that (in spite of his translation of Lucretius, his original *gassendisme,* and his various love affairs) he did not have a certain foundation of moderate and sensible religion, such as accorded with the cus-tom of the times—a religion which reappeared at his last hour, and of which there has been such a powerful burst from the lips of Cléante in *Tartuffe.* No, Molière the wise, an Ariste in his regard for the proprieties, the father of that Philinte whom Lélius, Erasmus, and Atticus would have recognised, had nothing of the licen-tious and cynical braggadocio of the Saint-Amants, Boisroberts, and Des Barreaux. He was

sincere in his indignation at the malicious in-
sinuations which, from the time he wrote his
École des Femmes, his enemies brought against
his religion.

What I seek to establish, and what distinguishes
him from the other geniuses among his contemporaries, is that he habitually saw human nature
as it is and always has been, in all its universality, as Boileau and La Bruyère saw and painted
it; but he did not give it Boileau's colouring in the *Épître sur l'Amour de Dieu,* nor La
Bruyère's in the Discussion on Quietism. He
paints humanity as if it had no growth, and he
could do this the more easily as he chiefly painted
its vices and defects; in tragedy one cannot so
easily do without Christianity. Molière separates humanity from the person of Jesus Christ,
or rather he shows us the depth of the one without thinking much of the other, and herein he
detaches himself from his age. In one of his
famous scenes he, without a thought of harm,
makes the Pauper say to Don Juan those words
which he afterwards was forced to retract, so
great was the storm they raised: "You spend
your life in praying to God, and you are dying
of hunger; take this money; I give it to you from
love of humanity." The benevolence and philan-
thropy of the eighteenth century, of D'Alembert,

Diderot and Holbach, can all be found in these
words. And it was again Molière who could
make the Pauper, on bringing back the gold piece,
say those other words so often quoted, but whose
deeper meaning, it seems to me, is so little understood—words that escaped a mind philosophic to
the core: "Where can virtue find a hiding
place?"—*Où la vertu va-t-elle se nicher?* No
denizen of Port-Royal or its vicinity (be it understood) would have had such a thought; the contrary, rather, would have seemed to him natural,
the poor man being, in the eyes of a good Christian, an object of special mercies and virtues. It
was Molière, too, who on discussing with Chapelle
the philosophy of Gassendi, their common master, said while they were disputing about the mys-
tery of the atomic theory: "Never mind the
morality of it." Molière had then, it seems to
me, simply the religion, I shall not say of Don
Juan or of Epicurus, but of Chremes in Terence:
Homo sum. We may apply to him in a serious
sense Tartuffe's remark: "A man . . . a man,
in short." This man knew what weaknesses
were, and was not surprised by them; he practised the good more than he believed in it; he expected vices, and his most burning indignation
turned into laughter. It pleased him to look upon
this sad humanity of ours as upon an old and in-

curable child, which must be corrected now and
then, but, above all, must be comforted by amusing
it.

To-day, as we look upon things from a distance
and can clearly survey results, Molière appears
to us much more radically aggressive in his attacks upon the society of his time than, as a matter of fact, he intended to be; this is a danger
we ought to guard against in judging him.
Among the illustrious contemporaries I just now
mentioned there is one, only one, and he the one
we should be least inclined to connect with our
poet, who nevertheless, like Molière, and even to
a greater degree than he, put into question the
very foundations of society, and who faced, without prejudices of any kind, birth, rank and wealth.
Pascal, for he is that audacious man, used, however, the ruin to which he would reduce everything
around him solely as an argument for clinging,
terror-stricken, to the pillar of the temple, and
for convulsively grasping the cross. They both,
Pascal and Molière, seem to us to-day the most
formidable witnesses against the society of their
time: Molière filling a vast space and reaching
the very edge of the religious enclosure, forag-
ing with his troupe over the entire field of the old
society, holding up to indiscriminate ridicule titled
conceit, conjugal inequality, captious hypocrisy,

often frightening, by the same stroke, legitimate subordination, true piety and the wedded state; Pascal, in the very heart of orthodoxy, causing in his own fashion the arches of the edifice to tremble by his cries of anguish and by the Samson-like force with which he grasped the sacred pillar. But while thus—it seems to us with a certain novelty and accuracy—establishing a connection between them, we must not ascribe to Molière a more deliberate intention to overthrow the existing order than to Pascal; we must even grant that less calculation entered into his view of the whole matter. Had Plautus any deliberate second thought in his mind when he ridiculed usury, prostitution, slavery and all the other vices and evil customs of ancient society?

When Molière appeared upon the scene, the time was exactly ripe for the liberty he gave himself.or availed himself of. Louis XIV, still young, supported him in all his bold attempts, as well as in his easy freedom, and protected him against attacks. In his *Tartuffe,* and also in the tirade of Don Juan against complacent hypocrisy, Molière foresaw, with his prophetic eye, the sad end of a noble reign; and at a time when it was not easy to do it, but when he knew it was useful to do so, he pointed his warning finger at the growing vice. Had he lived till 1685, till the

reign of Mme. de Maintenon was openly declared,
or had he lived even from 1673 to 1685, during
the glorious period of the ascendency of Bossuet,
he would doubtless have been less well protected,
and probably been finally persecuted. Be this as
it may, as we look upon that comprehensive, free,
natural and philosophic mind, indifferent to what
they were trying so hard to restore, we understand perfectly the ire of the religious oracles of
those days against Molière, the cruel severity of
expression with which Bossuet mocks in triumph
at the actor dying on the stage, that indignation
of even the wise Bourdaloue in his pulpit after
the production of *Tartuffe,* friend of Boileau
though he was. We can even conceive the naïve
terror of the Jansenist Baillet, who, in his *Juge-
ment des Savants,* begins his article on Molière
with these words: "Monsieur de Molière is one
of the most dangerous enemies of the church of
Jesus Christ that this age or this world has produced," etc. It is true, however, that some clerical men, more amiable and more worldly, were
less severe towards him. Père Rapin praised
Molière at considerable length in his *Recherches
sur la Poétique,* and took him to task only for his
carelessness in unravelling his plots. Bouhours
wrote an epitaph on him in pleasing and apprecia-
tive verse.

Molière was so thoroughly a *man* in the freest sense that he drew upon himself the anathemas of the haughty and would-be reforming philosophy, just as he had incurred those of the ruling episcopate. On four different counts—*L'Avare, Le Misanthrope, Georges Dandin* and *Le Bourgeois Gentilhomme*—Jean Jacques takes no joke, and spares Molière no more than Bossuet did.

With all this we have simply said that, like Shakespeare and Cervantes, like three or four supreme geniuses in the course of the ages, Molière is a painter of human nature to its depths, without acceptance of, or concern about, forms of worship, fixed dogma, or formal interpretation; that in attacking the society of his time he represented life as it is found among most of those around us; and that in the midst of established customs and morals, which he chastised to the quick, he is found to have written of all mankind.

.   .   .   .

In that company of great minds which includes, in different ages and in varying rank, Cervantes, Rabelais, Le Sage, Fielding, Beaumarchais and Walter Scott, Molière is, with Shakespeare, the most complete example of that dramatic and, properly speaking, creative faculty which I would fain describe with accuracy. Shakespeare has,

more than Molière, pathetic touches and flashes
of the terrible—witness Macbeth, King Lear and
Ophelia; but Molière compensates us in cértain
respects for this loss by the number, the perfection, the closely knit texture and the consistency
of his principal characters. Evidently in all the
great men, most of all in Molière, the dramatic
genius is not merely an expansion of their individual lyric faculty—an extraneous addition to
it, as it were—it is not a force which proceeding
from deep inner sentiments, laboriously trans-
ports them to an outer world in which they live,
in so far as it is possible, under strange masks
(as was the case with Byron in his tragedies);
nor is it the simple application of a faculty of
critical and analytic observation which sets off,
in the personages of an elaborate composition, the
various traits collected (like Gresset in *Le
Méchant*). There is a whole class of real dramatists who have something lyrical, one might almost say something blind, in their inspiration;
a warmth which springs from keen, inward sentiment, which they impart directly to their personages. Molière said of Corneille: "He has an
imp that comes to him from time to time to whisper excellent verses in his ear, and then leaves
him, saying: 'Now let us see how he will get on
without me.' And, true enough, he produces

nothing of any value, and the imp laughs and enjoys himself." Was it not in a similar sense, (and not as Voltaire would have it understood) that Richelieu reproached Corneille with not having had a "continuous intellect"—*l'esprit de suite?*

Crébillon, Schiller, Ducis, old Marlowe, were in their dramatic creativeness all subject to the visitation of such imps, to access of sudden emotion. They did not govern their genius with the fulness and consistency of free human beings. Often sublime and overpowering, they seem to obey the call of a certain instinct and a noble inner heat; like brave animals, lions or bulls, they know not fully what they are doing. Molière, like Shakespeare, does know; like his great predecessor, he moves, one may say, in a wider, freer, and therefore greater sphere; he governs himself, ardent in his work, but lucid in his ardour.

Nevertheless, this lucidity, this habitual coldness of character in the midst of such stirring work, had nothing of the calculated, icy impartiality of Goethe, that Talleyrand in his art—such critical subtleties, in the very bosom of poetry, had not as yet been invented. Molière and Shakespeare are two brothers of a primitive race, but with this difference, as it seems to me, that in his ordinary life Shakespeare, the poet who com-

manded tears and terror, found pleasure in culti-
vating a more smiling and a happier nature, while
Molière, the gay comedian, gave himself up, more
and more, to melancholy and silence.—*Portraits
Littéraires,* Essay on Molière.

GOETHE ON BÉRANGER

I

These songs are perfect and the best of their
kind, particularly if we add to them in imagination the melody of the refrain. Without this they
are, for songs, almost too serious, too pointed and
epigrammatic. Béranger always reminds me of
Horace and Hafiz, who rose above the foibles of
their time, and treated the prevailing immorality
mockingly and playfully. Béranger had the same
attitude towards his contemporaries, but as he
was of low birth, he was not too much incensed at
the licentious and vulgar, and treats it rather with
a certain partiality.

II

I am, on the whole, no admirer of so-called political poems, but such as Béranger has written I
can enjoy. With him there is nothing purely imaginary or fictitious, nothing spun out of thin air,
nothing aimless; but, on the contrary, his subjects
are always clear-cut and important. His affec-

tion and admiration for Napoleon and his remi-
niscences of his great deeds in war, reminis-
cences which at a period of depression proved a
source of consolation; his hatred of priest rule
and darkness, which threatened to return with the
Jesuits—these are all things with which one must
fully sympathise. And how masterly throughout
is the treatment of his subject! How he thinks
out and polishes everything before expressing
it! And where all is mature, what wit, spirit,
irony, and persiflage, what genuine feeling,
naïveté, grace, encounter us at every step! His
songs have given joy to millions of people year
after year; they flow freely from the lips of the
working classes, although they are so far above
the level of the commonplace that the people, in
communing with his charming creations, become
themselves nobler and better. Can you demand
more of a poet? And can there be higher praise
for his work?—*Eckermann's Conversations with
Goethe.*

SAINTE-BEUVE ON BÉRANGER

Béranger has certainly made of the *chanson* all
that can be made of it; he has drawn from it all
it contains, and one is inclined to believe that it
will henceforth be difficult to attempt anything
in this genre without imitating him. The spirit

of the old French song, light, mocking, satirical, disdaining a severer rhythm, has become transformed and more elevated; those who loved in these songs, above all, that French gaiety which knows how to be at the same time slightly malicious and inoffensive, have found that it lost some of its character in Béranger. In that naïve gaiety, that frank and complete *bonhomie,* the amiable Désaugiers is superior to him. Béranger, even as simple song-writer, has too much art, too much calculation, and too many tricks; he thinks of too many things at a time to be completely and innocently gay. He has pushed the song as far as it can go, and to the point where it ceases to be itself. This is his glory, but it implies a slight defect. Béranger has written songs, and more than songs; but has he written perfect odes? This is a literary question which has scarcely been touched upon before, so universally and loudly has Béranger been acclaimed a classic like Horace, and the only classic among living poets.

I have just re-read almost entirely (re-read, it is true, and not sung) the collected songs of Béranger and have arrived at the conviction that with him the original idea, the conception of the piece is almost always charming and poetic, but that the execution, because of the difficulties of

the rhythm and of the refrain, because, furthermore, of certain literary peculiarities inherent in
him, or characteristic of the time, is often not
faultless. . . .

Le Roi d' Yvetot, by which he made his début
in May, 1813, seems to me perfect; there is not
a word which is not to the point, which is not part
of the rhythm and in keeping with the rest; everything is poetic, natural and gay. The happy
rhyme and jest are in perfect accord with the
sense and spirit of the whole. . . .

To sum up: Béranger is one of the greatest
poets of our age, but he is not the greatest. The
difference between the ranks is not, in my opinion,
as clear-cut as his exclusive admirers believe.
There are various admixtures in his much-lauded
perfection. Compared with poets of a former
time, he belongs to the second group, still rare
enough, which includes a Burns, a Horace, a La
Fontaine. But these, who were never poets of a
party, retain for this very reason a higher rank
and belong to a more universally human order.
Read Horace in his Epistles, La Fontaine in his
Fables: they flatter no passion, they fondle no
human folly. If Béranger castigated more than
one, he has caressed too many others. In the end,
Béranger seems to me to have come to the same
conclusion as Voltaire, as Rabelais, as Cervantes:

that there are more fools than wise men in the world—more fools, as he says, than knaves. But is this observation made sufficiently clear in his works, and does it not often seem, in reading him, as if all the wisdom, all sound reason, were on one side, and all wrong and all unreason on the other? That fixed belief in the wisdom and the infallible virtues of the masses detracts greatly from his merit, in my opinion. But he has succeeded in an age of restless strife and selfish effort, in finding a new vein. His poetry, that masterly, living, sensitive, elevated, roguish, original poetry, has flowed forth in a constant stream, and he is sufficiently pre-eminent to be sure of surviving, even after some of the passions to which he ministered, and which are not immortal, shall have expired. —*Causeries du Lundi,* Vol. II, "Chansons de Béranger."

LOWELL ON BÉRANGER

I

The Roman genius was eminently practical, and far more apt for the triumphs of politics and jurisprudence than of art. Supreme elegance it could and did arrive at in Virgil, but, if I may trust my own judgment, it produced but one original poet, and that was Horace, who has ever since continued the favourite of men of the world, an apostle to the Gentiles of the mild cynicism of middle-age and an after-dinner philosophy. Though in no sense national, he was, more truly than any has even been since, till the same combination of circumstances produced Béranger, an urbane or city poet.—*Essay on Chaucer.*

II

I would not be supposed to overlook the distinction, too often lost sight of, between sentimentalism and sentiment, the latter being a very excellent thing in its way, as genuine things are apt to be. Sentiment is intellectualised emotion, emotion precipitated, as it were, in pretty crystals by the fancy. This is the delightful staple of the poets of social life like Horace and Béranger, or Thackeray, when he too rarely played with verse. —*Rousseau and the Sentimentalists.*

GOETHE ON ROUSSEAU

I

I cannot but agree with your remarks concerning Rousseau's *Pygmalion.* It is indeed a monstrous production and most significant as a symptom of the principal malady of a time when State, art, and talent, together with a nameless something, which it was the fashion to call nature, was stirred and whipped up into a kind of stew. This operation I trust I shall make clear in my next volume; for was I not myself seized by the prevailing epidemic, and did not this fact favour my development, which I cannot conceive to have been possible in any other way?—*Letter to Zelter,* December 3, 1812.

II

To a youth of Klinger's nature Rousseau's work made a powerful appeal. *Émile* was his principal guide, and its sentiments, which exercise such an influence upon the whole civilised world, affected him even more than others. For he too was the child of nature, he too had risen from humble beginnings . . . he could therefore be regarded as one of the purest disciples of that gospel of nature, and in view of his serious endeavours and his deportment, as man and son, he might well exclaim: "All is good as it leaves the hand of nature!" But the conclusion, "All is good as it leaves the hand of man," was also forced upon him by adverse fate. He had no inward struggles, but found himself engaged in combating the world of conventions, from whose fetters the Citizen of Geneva had hoped to free us. —*Autobiography,* Part III, Book XIV.

III

I must mention a work small in compass, but epoch making to an extraordinary degree—I mean Rousseau's *Pygmalion*. Much might be said about it: for this strange production hovers between nature and art in the mistaken effort to turn art into nature. We have before us an artist who has produced a work of the greatest perfection, and yet has found no satisfaction in giving his idea artistic shape and endowing it with a higher life. He drags it back to the level of his own earthly life; he must destroy the highest production of mind and hand by the most vulgar act of sensuality.—*Autobiography*, Part III, Book XI.

GRILLPARZER ON ROUSSEAU

1822

How surprised Rousseau would have been if any one had called him the most complete egotist that ever lived! A man who liked in all those with whom he came in contact merely the ideas which he could associate with them, but never the persons themselves; who therefore never had a real friend, nor ever found a woman who truly loved him; who put his children into the foundling hospital because they interfered with the life plan he had mapped out for himself, and was ever after utterly indifferent to their fate; who, in order to remain unfettered, kept the woman who showed such devotion for him as his mistress, instead of rendering her happy by the name of wife; who considered himself the centre of creation, and all that happened around him merely as having happened for his sake; who, if an earthquake or the sudden eruption of a volcano had disturbed him in writing, would have looked upon it as a conspiracy against his person; whose desire for distinction was so great that because he could not possess all the outward tokens of it alone, preferred to renounce distinction altogether; who despised the world because he did not know how to live in it; despised society because he could not adapt himself to its tone; who sought solitude because in it he found what alone interested him in this world—himself, his thoughts and emotions. If all this had been told him by some one who at the same time professed brotherly sentiments, what would he have answered? He would never have believed him, though all of what I have said is true—without necessarily implying that Rousseau was morally the worse for it. His condition was that of a being completely dominated by his thoughts. He believed that he was controlled by his emotions, but the reverse was the case; his emotions invariably resulted from his thoughts,

and from them alone. Whatever offered no
scope to his ideas did not touch his emotions, as
witness his children, who crossed his plans, and
therefore had to be taken out of his way. Never
did he speak a truer word of himself than when
he said: "I must be left to my thoughts if I am
to love" (J'ai besoin de me recueillir pour
aimer), and herein lies the key to his life. He
who abandons himself completely to his thoughts,
particularly in solitude, will find that they swal-
low up the whole world, feeding everywhere on
the nourishment they crave, and finally leaving
him who is their prey alone in an empty and joy-
less desert.*

The twelfth book of Rousseau's *Confessions*
appears to me strikingly different from the preceding ones. It seems as though the author, fatigued by his long labours, had forgotten the poetic view of his life and the consistent dramatic
development of the character which he had
adopted for himself, and had suddenly dropped
into the prose of reality. His vanity, and the desire ever to distinguish himself by peculiarities
of behaviour are all too evident. Everywhere
there are traces of *ennui*. One feels that he is describing the present, which, naturally, is not so
easy to idealise as the past.

1859

Rousseau probably believed that in his *Nouvelle Héloise* he was writing principally a work of sentiment. And it is indeed full of sentiments, but one is lacking, and that the mother of all the rest —the sense of shame, and Rousseau himself, in spite of his great gifts, and although he probably imagined himself a sort of Saint-Preux, was nothing but a sort of Wolmar.

———

Rousseau, in his *Émile*, admits that he was wrong in sending his three children to the foundling hospital; it is comical to see that he imagined that this confession absolved him once for all from all guilt, and that henceforth it would be wrong to charge him with it. He was a pure *amateur* in matters of virtue.

SAINTE-BEUVE ON ROUSSEAU

I

After speaking of the pure, light, graceful, wholly smooth and fluent language which the closing seventeenth century had partly bequeathed to the eighteenth, I should like to speak to-day of this language of the eighteenth century, as revealed in the writer to whom it owed its greatest progress, and through whom it underwent the

greatest revolution since Pascal, a revolution
from which we writers of the nineteenth century
date our beginning. Before Rousseau and since
Fénelon, there had been efforts to create various
styles of writing which were no longer those of
the seventeenth century in its greatest purity.
Fontenelle had his manner, if ever there was a
manner; Montesquieu had his, more pronounced,
firmer, more striking, but a manner nevertheless.
Voltaire alone had no manner, and his speech,
lively, clear and rapid, flowed as if directly from
the source. "You find," he writes somewhere,
"that I express myself clearly: I am like the
little brooks which are transparent because shallow." He said this laughingly. One often tells
himself half-truths of this kind. The age, however, demanded more; it wanted to be moved,
warmed, rejuvenated by the expression of ideas
and sentiments which it could not well define and
was still groping for. Buffon's prose, in the
first volume of the *Natural History,* offered the
age some image of what it was yearning for, an
image more majestic than real, almost beyond
reach and too closely allied to scientific subjects.
Rousseau appeared on the scene. On the day
when he first found himself he revealed at the
same time to his century the writer who was best
fitted to express with novelty, with power, and

with fiery logic, the confused ideas struggling to see the light. In using as his own the language which he had had to conquer and to master, he forced it here and there, and gave it a stamp which it was destined to bear henceforth; but he gave to it more than it lost, and in many respects he gave it a new life and a new might. Into the form of the language created and established by him our greatest writers have since thrown their own innovations and attempted improvements. The pure form of the seventeenth century, which we love to recall, has hardly been more than a graceful relic of antiquity, which persons of good taste nowadays look back upon regretfully.

II

The first book of the *Confessions* is not the most remarkable, but it reveals to us already the whole of Rousseau, with his pride, his budding vices, his queer and grotesque humours, his meanness, and his unclean actions; with his nobler pride too, and that spirit of independence and strength which lifts him up again; with his happy and healthy childhood, his suffering and tortured youth, which drew from him later on (we already feel their approach) those tirades against society and that spiteful revenge. We see him with his tender sense of domestic happiness and family life of

which he was to know so little, and those first
breezes, signs of the natural awakening which so
brilliantly ushered in the literature of the nineteenth century. We are in danger to-day of ap-
preciating too little these first picturesque pages of
Rousseau; we have become so spoiled by brighter
colours that we forget how fresh and new those
early landscapes appeared at the time, and what
an event they formed in the midst of that society,
full of wit and refinement but barren withal, as
devoid of imagination as of real sentiment, destitute of that circulating sap which at every season
flowers anew. Rousseau was the first to bring
back and infuse that powerful vivifying fluid into
a nearly exhausted tree. French readers accustomed to the artificial atmosphere of the *salon*,
those urban readers as he calls them, feel with rap-
tured astonishment those fresh and healthy mountain breezes, which, coming from the Alps,
revived a literature as famous as it was sapless.

III

The mistake of Rousseau was not in believing
that by proclaiming his profession aloud to all the
world, and with a feeling so different from Christian humility, he was doing an unique thing or even
a thing of the greatest interest as regards the
state of the human heart; his mistake lay in be-

lieving that he was doing a useful thing. He did
not see that he was acting like a physician who
places before the whole world, the wise and ignorant alike, a description of a characteristic mental
malady; such a physician would be partly and
justly responsible for all the fools and maniacs
whom his books might teach to imitate the folly
which it describes. *Causeries du Lundi,* Vol. III,
"Les Confessions de J. J. Rousseau."

LOWELL ON ROUSSEAU

I

Rousseau has, in one respect, been utterly mis-
represented and misunderstood. Even Chateaubriand most unfilially classes him and Voltaire
together. It appears to me that the inmost core
of his being was religious. Had he remained in
the Catholic Church, he might have been a saint.
Had he come earlier, he might have founded an
order. His was precisely the nature on which religious enthusiasm takes the strongest hold, a temperament which finds sensuous delight in spiritual
things, and satisfies its craving for excitement
with celestial debauch. He had not the iron temper of a great reformer and organiser like Knox,
who, true Scotchman that he was, found a way to

weld this world and the other together in a cast-
iron creed; but he had as much as any man ever
had that gift of a great preacher to make the ora-
torical fervour which persuades himself while it
lasts into the abiding conviction of his hearers.
That very persuasion of his, that the soul could
remain pure while the life was corrupt, is not un-
exampled among men who have left holier names
than he. His *Confessions,* also, would assign him
to that class with whom the religious sentiment is
strong and the moral nature weak. They are apt
to believe that they may, as special pleaders say,
confess and avoid. Hawthorne had admirably
illustrated this in the penance of Mr. Dimmesdale.
With all the soil that is upon Rousseau, I cannot
help looking on him as one capable beyond any in
his generation of being divinely possessed; and if
it happened otherwise, when we remember the
much that hindered and the little that helped in a
life and time like his, we shall be much readier to
pity than to condemn. It was his very fitness for
being something better that makes him able to
shock us so with what in too many respects he
unhappily was. Less gifted, he had been less
hardly judged. More than any other of the sentimentalists, except possibly Sterne, he had in him
a staple of sincerity. Compared with Chateau-

briand, he is honesty, compared with Lamartine, he is manliness, itself. His nearest congener in our own tongue is Cowper.

II

In nearly all that he wrote his leading object was the good of his kind, and that, through all the vicissitudes of a life which illness, sensibility of temperament, and the approaches of insanity rendered wretched,—the associate of infidels, the foundling child, as it were, of an age without belief, least of all with any belief in itself,—he professed and evidently felt deeply a faith in the goodness both of man and of God. There is no such thing as scoffing in his writings. On the other hand, there is no stereotyped morality. He does not ignore the existence of scepticism; he recognises its existence in his own nature, meets it frankly face to face, and makes it confess that there are things in the teaching of Christ that are deeper than its doubt. The influence of his early education at Geneva is apparent here. An intellect so acute as his, trained in the school of Calvin in a republic where theological discussion was as much the amusement of the people as the opera was at Paris, could not fail to be a good logician. He had the fortitude to follow his logic wherever it led him. If the very impressibility of character which quickened his perception of the beauties of nature, and made him alive to the charm of music and musical expression, prevented him from being in the highest sense an original writer, and if his ideas were mostly suggested to him by books, yet the clearness, consecutiveness, and eloquence with which he stated and enforced them made them his own. There was at least that original fire in him which could fuse them and run them in a novel mould. His power lay in this very ability of manipulating the thoughts of others. Fond of paradox he doubtless was, but he had a way of putting things that arrested attention and excited thought.

III

It strikes me as a little singular that one whose life was so full of moral inconsistency, whose character is so contemptible in many ways, in some one might almost say so revolting, should yet have exercised so deep and lasting an influence, and on minds so various, should still be an object of minute and earnest discussion,—that he should have had such vigour in his intellectual loins as to have been the father of Chateaubriand, Byron, Lamartine, George Sand, and many more in literature, in politics of Jefferson and Thomas Paine,— that the spots he had haunted should draw pil-

grims so unlike as Gibbon and Napoleon, nay,
should draw them still, after the lapse of near a
century. Surely there must have been a basis of
sincerity in this man seldom matched, if it can
prevail against so many reasons of repugnance,
aversion, and even disgust. He could not have
been the mere sentimentalist and rhetorician for
which the rough-and-ready understanding would
at first glance be inclined to condemn him. In a
certain sense he was both of these, but he was
something more.—*Rousseau and the Sentimentalists.*

GRILLPARZER ON VICTOR HUGO

1834

Journal des idées d'un jeune royaliste.—This
collection begins with the sixteenth year of the
author. The views of a celebrated writer concerning literary and artistic matters, even if relating
to so early a period of his life, may conceivably be
of interest; but his political opinions at such a time
are absolutely valueless. Hugo speaks of form
and style as the first prerequisite of a great work
of art, and of the contents as the second. This,
to say the least, strikes me as very queer. Is not
what an author treats of more important than
how he treats it? And yet he maintains that the

object of art is purely practical, and that is his principal fault, as well as that of the entire modern French school. "Il pense (le vrai poète) qu'au théâtre surtout il ne suffit pas de remplir seulement les conditions de l'art." What else is the object of the stage?

"Le théâtre est une chose qui enseigne et qui civilise." Why not? That is to say, indirectly and incidentally, but to teach directly and of set purpose is the most inartistic procedure imaginable.

"L'art d' à présent ne doit plus chercher seulement le beau, mais encore le bien." But wherein lies the difference between prose and poetry if the object of both is the same? Fortunately, he immediately contradicts himself and says that the dramatic author is to civilise and edify "chemin faisant, sans se détourner et tout en allant devant lui."

"On nomme *action* au théâtre la lutte de deux forces opposées." There is sense in that. While it does not apply to every case, it is on the whole about the best definition of the term "action" which I have ever come across.

"Plus ces forces se contrebalancent, plus la lutte est incertaine, plus il y a alternative de crainte ou d'espérance, plus il y a d'intérêt." This is good.

"Il ne faut pas confondre cet intérêt, qui naît

de l'action avec une autre sorte d'intérêt, que doit inspirer le héros de toute tragédie, et qui n'est qu'un sentiment de terreur, d'admiration ou de pitié." The first part of the sentence is very true, but the second is badly expressed. "Terreur, pitié" are sentiments which accompany action; before the hero acts he can only excite love, aversion, admiration or hatred.

"Ainsi il se pourrait très-bien que le principal personnage d'une pièce excitât de l'intérêt, parce que son caractère est noble et sa situation touchante, et que la piece manquât d'intérêt, parce qu'il n'y aurait point d'alternative de crainte et d'espérance." There is in *Lear* no such alternative, and yet the play does not lack interest. On the whole, however, Hugo is right.

In comparing Le Sage and Walter Scott he seems to be inclined to give the preference to the latter. I fear posterity will be of the opposite opinion, at least as far as *Gil Blas* is concerned.

André Chénier, to judge from the specimens quoted, is indeed a poet and a greater one than any now living. He may be said to be a model upon which Lamartine formed his lyrics, and thus, through Lamartine, Victor Hugo his own poetry.

The thoughts of a revolutionary of 1830 ought, if printed at all, not to be printed upon such beautiful paper and with such lavish display of space.

Sur Voltaire. "Son poème blafard de la Ligue, depuis la Henriade . . . et son remarquable drame d'Œdipe"—two curious adjectives in this juxtaposition.

A better contrast is that between Frederick II and Voltaire; "le despote—philosophe et le sophiste—poète."

It is not becoming in a young man to talk so disparagingly of subjects like the *Encyclopédie.* The whole essay is very immature.

SAINTE-BEUVE ON VICTOR HUGO

A man who for thirty years has occupied one of the foremost ranks in French poetry, and who has himself passed through many phases, has during that long time seen more than one group, more than one colony, of disciples and imitators attach themselves to him and, in turn, renounce him. There are among them some who have never been able to follow Victor Hugo beyond his first *Odes et Ballades,* and who imagined that from the day he wrote differently he wrote worse. There are some who followed him as far as the *Orientales* and no further; and there are some who went as far as the *Feuilles d' Automne,* and who still believe that when he wrote this work he was in his fullest and most beautiful maturity. In his dramas, too, there are steps beyond which certain

admirers did not venture. There are, on the other
hand, others who, according as they approached
him, in a spirit of youthful impetuosity or perhaps with sober reflection and calculation, started
precisely with those works of the famous poet that
marked the extreme point beyond which their
elders could not go. Théophile Gautier, who has
become chief of an important sub-division of the
partly dismembered school of Hugo, is among
those who were not afraid at the outset to borrow from the talent which was their source that
which to others seemed an excess or a limitation.
Wielding a skilful pen, master of colouring and of
subtle nuances, seeking art for art's sake, having
less to say than to describe, he has achieved in his
genre wonders of skill and of boldness; he has
made our language express more than it could
before his advent. His manner is a mannerism, if
there ever was one; but it is his own and he plays
with it. Maxime du Camp, with less finish, at-
taches himself by the side of Théophile Gautier to
the school of Victor Hugo; he loves and cultivates
description for its own sake, and goes in search of
it; one of his first objects has been to visit that
Orient of which his master has sung only from a
distance and upon the strength of a dream.—
Causeries du Lundi, Vol. XII, "Les Chants Mod-
ernes."

earth, and to remodel laws of art which are as unchangeable as those of astronomy, can do no very great harm to any one but the author himself, who will thereby be led astray from his proper function, and from the only path to legitimate and lasting success.—*The Life and Letters of James Gates Percival.*

III

There is something in Webster that reminds me of Victor Hugo.   There is the same confusion at times of what is big with what is great, the same fondness for the merely spectacular, the same insensibility to repulsive details, the same indifference to the probable or even to the natural, the same leaning toward the grotesque, the same love of effect at whatever cost; and there is also the same impressiveness of result.—*The Old English Dramatists,* Essay on Webster.

GERMAN LITERATURE

GOETHE ON LESSING

When critics compare the plays of Lessing with those of the ancients and pronounce them wretched, what are we to say? We can only pity that extraordinary man for having lived in a barren age which could give him no better subjects than those he made use of in his plays. Pitiful indeed is it that in his *Minna von Barnhelm* he had to take sides in the struggles between Saxons and Prussians, simply because he could find nothing better to write about. His incessant polemic activity was also due to the wretchedness of the times. In his *Emilia Galotti* he had his fling at princes, in his *Nathan,* at priests.—*Eckermann's Conversations with Goethe.*

GRILLPARZER ON LESSING

1849

I have read for the second time *Minna von Barnhelm*. What an admirable play! Evidently the best German comedy. A comedy? Yes, a comedy; why not? So thoroughly German in all its characters, and therefore unique in German literature. No French blustering humbug of a serv-

ant as a confidant of his master, but just the un-
couth, straightforward German Just. The inn-
keeper indeed is a specimen of the average man of
his kind, but how characteristic is Franziska!
How talkative and pert, and yet deliciously good
and honest and modest! Not a trace in her of the
French chambermaid, to whom the German ones
owe their origin, in life and on the stage. Minna
is glorious from the very beginning. If we were
to analyse this character we could not find any
single trait of which we could say in advance:
"This is going to be effective on the stage," and
yet in spite of it, or perhaps because of it, the
whole is so life-like—nothing evolved from a mere
idea. It is true that towards the end Minna's actions are not quite in keeping with her character,
but to come to wrong conclusions under the stress
of complications is human, as witness even Molière
in similar situations.

———

Lessing's chief merit lies in the combination of
his artistic sense with his logical acumen. It is
true his artistic sense is not always of the purest,
nor his logic the most flawless, but it is possible that both were never united before in such
perfection. As a rule, they are mutually exclusive.

1851

It has become customary to say that our literature dates from Lessing. This is not correct.
The father of our literature is Klopstock; he was
the first to throw a spark of inspiration into the
dull and pedantic masses, and only as one between
Klopstock and Goethe, with Wieland at his side,
can Lessing be hailed as our saviour. It must be
admitted that the man's love of truth was not free
from quarrelsomeness, nor his criticism free from
envy. Instead of receiving Klopstock with open
arms as the only German poet, he constantly found
fault with him; Wieland's enjoyment of his own
harmless productions was an eyesore to him, and
he did not recognise the value of Goethe's first
creations. His friendship for Ramler and Nicolai
throws some light on his critical attitude. When
he attacked the faults of the French tragic poets,
the blunt frankness of his nature was enlisted as
much as his critical acumen. This æsthetic and
logical conviction led him to welcome far inferior
kinds of dramas, such as lachrymose comedies and
philistine tragedies. His devotion to Shakespeare
could not save him from imitating Diderot. With
all this, I do not wish to deny Lessing's infinite
merit; my object is merely to protest against the
blind adoration of him on the part of those who
imagine they see a resemblance between him and

themselves, and who praise themselves in prais-
ing him. Lessing's chief value lies in being the
greatest writer of a kind which is in itself open to
objection; those nearest to him in degree are
merely swaggerers or prosy writers who try to
poetise.

LOWELL ON LESSING

I

My respect for what Lessing was, and for what
he did, is profound.   In the history of literature it
would be hard to find a man so stalwart, so kindly,
so sincere, so capable of great ideas, whether in
their influence on the intellect or the life, so un-
swervingly true to the truth, so free from the common weaknesses of his class.   Since Luther, Germany has given birth to no such intellectual ath-
lete, no son so German to the core.   Greater poets
she has had, but no greater writer; no nature more
finely tempered.   Nay, may we not say that great
character is as rare a thing as great genius, if it
be not even a nobler form of it?   For surely it is
easier to embody fine thinking, or delicate sentiment, or lofty aspiration, in a book than in a life.
The written leaf, if it be, as some few are, a safe-
keeper and conductor of celestial fire, is secure.
Poverty cannot pinch, passion swerve, or trial
shake it.   But the man Lessing, harassed and

striving life-long, always poor and always hope-
ful, with no patron but his own right-hand, the
very shuttlecock of fortune, who saw ruin's
ploughshare drive through the hearth on which his
first home-fire was hardly kindled, and who,
through all, was faithful to himself, to his friend,
to his duty, and to his ideal, is something more
inspiring for us than the most glorious utterance
of merely intellectual power. The figure of
Goethe is grand, it is rightfully pre-eminent, it has
something of the calm, and something of the coldness, of the immortals; but the Valhalla of German letters can show one form, in its simple manhood, statelier even than his.

II

As an author, Lessing began his career at a period when we cannot say that German literature was
at its lowest ebb, only because there had not yet
been any flood-tide.   That may be said to have begun with him.   When we say German literature,
we mean so much of it as has any interest outside
of Germany.   That part of the literary histories
which treats of the dead waste and middle of the
eighteenth century reads like a collection of obitu-
aries, and were better reduced to the conciseness
of epitaph, though the authors of them seem to find
a melancholy pleasure, much like that of under-

takers, in the task by which they live. Gottsched
reigned supreme on the legitimate throne of dulness. In Switzerland, Bodmer essayed a more re-
publican form of the same authority. At that
time a traveller reports eight hundred authors in
Zürich alone! Young aspirant for lettered fame,
in imagination clear away the lichens from their
forgotten headstones, and read humbly the "As I
am, so thou must be," on all! Everybody remembers how Goethe, in the seventh book of his autobiography, tells the story of his visit to Gottsched.
He enters by mistake an inner room at the moment
when a frightened servant brings the discrowned
potentate a periwig large enough to reach to the
elbows. That awful emblem of pretentious sham
seems to be the best type of the literature then pre-
dominant. We always fancy it set upon a pole,
like Gessler's hat, with nothing in it that was not
wooden, for all men to bow down before. The
periwig style had its natural place in the age of
Louis XIV., and there were certainly brains under
it. But it had run out in France, as the tie-wig
style of Pope had in England. In Germany it was
the mere imitation of an imitation. Will it be
believed that Gottsched recommends his *Art of
Poetry* to beginners, in preference to Breitinger's,
because it *"will enable them to produce every
species of poem in a correct style,* while out of that

no one can learn to make an ode or a cantata''?
''Whoever,'' he says, ''buys Breitinger's book *in
order to learn how to make poems,* will too late
regret his money.'' Gottsched, perhaps, did some
service even by his advocacy of French models,
by calling attention to the fact that there *was* such
a thing as style, and that it was of some conse-
quence. But not one of the authors of that time
can be said to survive, nor to be known even by
name except to Germans, unless it be Klopstock,
Herder, Wieland, and Gellert. And the latter's
immortality, such as it is, reminds us somewhat of
that Lady Gosling's, whose obituary stated that
she was ''mentioned by Mrs. Barbauld in her *Life
of Richardson* 'under the name of Miss M., afterwards Lady G.' '' Klopstock himself is rather remembered for what he was than what he is,—an
immortality of preteriteness; and we much doubt
if many Germans put the *Oberon* in their trunks
when they start on a journey. Herder alone survives, if not as a contributor to literature, strictly
so called, yet as a thinker and as part of the intellectual impulse of the day. But at the time,
though there were two parties, yet within the lines
of each there was a loyal reciprocity of what is
called on such occasions appreciation. Wig
ducked to wig, each blockhead had a brother, and
there was a universal apotheosis of the mediocrity

of our set.   If the greatest happiness of the greatest number be the true theory, this was all that
could be desired.   Even Lessing at one time
looked up to Hagedorn as the German Horace.   If
Hagedorn were pleased, what mattered it to Horace?   Worse almost than this was the universal
pedantry.   The solemn bray of one pedagogue
was taken up and prolonged in a thousand echoes.
There was not only no originality, but no desire
for it,—perhaps even a dread of it, as something
that would break the *entente cordiale* of placid
mutual assurance.   No great writer had given
that tone of good-breeding to the language which
would gain it entrance to the society of European
literature.   No man of genius had made it a necessity of polite culture.   It was still as rudely provincial as the Scotch of Allan Ramsay.   Frederick the Great was to be forgiven if, with his
practical turn, he gave himself wholly to French,
which had replaced Latin as a cosmopolitan
tongue.   It had lightness, ease, fluency, elegance,
lucidity—in short, all the good qualities that German lacked.   The study of French models was
perhaps the best thing for German literature before it got out of long-clothes.   It was bad only
when it became a tradition and a tyranny.   Lessing did more than any other man to overthrow
this foreign usurpation when it had done its work,

III

It is a striking illustration at once of the futility of mere critical insight and of Lessing's want of imagination, that in the *Emilia* he should have thought a Roman motive consistent with modern habits of thought, and that in *Nathan* he should have been guilty of anachronisms which violate not only the accidental truth of fact, but the essential truth of character. Even if we allowed him imagination, it must be only on the lower plane of prose; for of verse as anything more than so many metrical feet he had not the faintest notion. Of that exquisite sympathy with the movement of the mind, with every swifter or slower pulse of passion, which proves it another species from prose, the very αφροδίτη καὶ λύρα of speech, and not merely a higher form of it, he wanted the fineness of sense to conceive. If we compare the prose of Dante or Milton, though both were eloquent, with their verse, we see at once which was the more congenial to them. Lessing has passages of freer and more harmonious utterance in some of his most careless prose esays, than can be found in his *Nathan* from the first line to the last. In the *numeris lege solutis* he is often snatched beyond himself, and becomes truly dithyrambic; in his pentameters the march of the thought is comparatively hampered and irresolute. His best things are not poetically delicate, but have the tougher fibre of proverbs. Is it not enough, then, to be a great prose-writer? They are as rare as great poets, and if Lessing have the gift to stir and to dilate that something deeper than the mind which genius only can reach, what matter if it be not done to music? Of his minor poems I need say little. Verse was always more or less mechanical with him, and his epigrams are almost all stiff, as if they were bad translations from the Latin. Many of them are shockingly coarse, and in liveliness are on a level with those of our Elizabethan period.

IV

It is not without reason that fame is awarded only after death. The dust-cloud of notoriety which follows and envelops the men who drive with the wind bewilders contemporary judgment. Lessing, while he lived, had little reward for his labour but the satisfaction inherent in all work faithfully done; the highest, no doubt, of which human nature is capable, and yet perhaps not so sweet as that sympathy of which the world's praise is but an index. But if to perpetuate herself beyond the grave in healthy and ennobling influences be the noblest aspiration of the mind, and its fruition the only reward she would have deemed worthy of herself, then is Lessing to be counted thrice fortunate. Every year since he was laid prematurely in the earth has seen his power for good increase, and made him more precious to the hearts and intellects of men.— *Essay on Lessing*.

GOETHE ON SCHILLER

I

Everything else about him was proud and majestic, but his eyes were gentle. And as his talent was, so was his outward form. He seized boldly upon a great subject, looking upon it from all sides and turning it about this way and that. Yet he saw his subject, as it were, only from the outside, and it was not in his nature to develop it quietly from within. His talent was in some respects desultory; therefore he could not easily come to a decision, and seemed never to be able to finish. He often changed a part just before the rehearsal.

And going boldly to work as he did, he did not trouble himself much about motives. I recollect how I had to argue with him about the scene in *William Tell* where he originally intended to let Gessler suddenly pluck an apple from the tree and shoot it off the head of Tell's boy. Such a procedure was wholly against my nature, and I per-

suaded him to give at least some motive for this
cruelty by making the boy boast to Gessler of his
father's skill and say that he could shoot an
apple from a tree at a distance of a hundred paces.
Schiller at first would have none of this; but he
yielded at last to my arguments and did as I ad-
vised him. . . .

Schiller's genius was eminently adapted for the
theatre. He progressed towards perfection with
every new play; but, strange to say, he retained
from the time of his *Robbers* a certain fondness
for the cruel, which did not wholly leave him after
he had reached his zenith. I remember well that
in the prison scene in my *Egmont,* where the sentence is read to him, Schiller wished me to let
Alva, masked and muffled, appear in the background, enjoying the effect produced by the death
sentence upon Egmont. Alva was thereby to
show himself insatiable in his malice and revenge-
fulness. I protested, however, and the apparition
was not introduced. Schiller was great indeed,
though not free from oddities. He seemed to
change from week to week and to become more and
more complete. Whenever I saw him he appeared
to me more advanced in learning and riper in
judgment.—*Eckermann's   Conversations   with
Goethe.*

II

It was not in Schiller's nature to work without conscious effort and, as it were, instinctively; he had to reflect upon all he undertook to do. He therefore could not refrain from discussing in detail all his poetic projects. He talked over with me all his later plays, scene by scene. My nature was entirely different. I never talked with any one about my poetic plans, not even with Schiller. I kept my ideas to myself, and as a rule no one knew what I was planning until it was all finished. When I showed Schiller my *Hermann und Dorothea,* he was completely taken by surprise, for I had not told him a syllable of what I was doing.— *Eckermann's Conversations with Goethe.*

GRILLPARZER ON SCHILLER

If one could only eliminate the two monologues of Elizabeth and Leicester in *Maria Stuart!* It is Schiller's greatest fault that he speaks too often himself instead of allowing his characters to speak. Even the monologues of Wallenstein spoil much of the good impression previously created. It is, however, easier to criticise such things than to do better one's self. He who knows how innumerable are the threads that cross and recross each other in the handling of a vast dramatic web, will easily forgive the author if now and then a few slip through his fingers.

GRILLPARZER ON GOETHE

1832

With advancing age, but perhaps even more through the bureaucratic activity of his last years, Goethe lost much of that vivifying and visualising power which alone creates images and awakens emotions. The characters which he had endowed with all the wealth of his youth had faded into dreams and bloodless shadows, which may still, in some respects, command our admiration, but toward which we are no longer drawn by real sympathy. Perhaps we might say that in his last days Goethe had a natural desire to leave none of the children of his intellect unprovided for. . . . He was thus impelled to weld together certain parts and fragments originally never intended for each other's company, and he left the care of providing for the unity of the whole to the admiration of future generations and to the magic of his name.*

1835

We hear the endless cry: "Goethe! Goethe!" There are so many forms of the man, which do you prefer? All—Goethe the youth, Goethe the man, the mature; yes, the over-ripe. After all, the differences between his many forms are not greater than those between the peach blossom and the peach itself, which show scarcely any resemblance and yet delight us equally. "Hoch auf dem alten Thurme steht" ("On high in th' ancient tower stands") is considered one of the most beautiful of Goethe's poems. Why not? It is, if the reader happens to be in the mood to make it beautiful to himself. The principal fault of Goethe's lyric poems is that they expect the reader to put himself, by conscious effort, in the position in which the poet was when he wrote them, and that they thus presuppose a certain mood instead of awakening it.

GRILLPARZER ON GOETHE'S "ELECTIVE AFFINITIES"

What is most disturbing in the *Wahlverwandtschaften* is the offensive importance given from the very beginning to the laying out of the park, the petty architectural details, and other things of this kind—an importance equal to that of the main incidents. We feel as though we were reading a chapter from the life of Goethe himself, who partially paralysed his incomparable gifts by taking almost as much interest in such pastimes as in the most important concerns of his real life. There must be a gradation of interest, and what is lavished on minor incidents is by so much withdrawn from the main action. By such spinning out of details, he, moreover, deprived himself of the necessary space in which to transform the purely mechanical element of his *Wahlverwandtschaften* into the psychological or, rather, moral. Women like Charlotte do not transfer their affections at a bound, and many steps in the scale of events and emotions are required until women like Ottilie turn even in thought to misconduct or sin. . . . But granted all this, what a wonderful masterpiece this work is! As regards knowledge of human nature, wisdom, depth of sentiment, power of description, character drawing, and poetic idealisation of the apparently commonplace, no literature can show its equal. Before one has reached the age of fifty, one can scarcely fully appreciate it, but it is as much a part of the curse as of the blessing of the years of maturity that one can appreciate it then. If I could claim its authorship as a gift, I should not care to have written it. The passionate exaltation of a Byron may perhaps transcend all limits—and, indeed, poetry derives its very being from the over-stepping of all bounds—but the nearer any literary work is to actual life, the more is it bound to respect that without which life is an abomination and a horror.*

GRILLPARZER APROPOS OF "ECKERMANN'S CONVERSATIONS WITH GOETHE"

1832

We have here again a collection of remarks by Goethe, which, like everything that concerns this extraordinary man, is of inestimable value—of value, that is to say, to those endowed with insight, but dangerous to those who lack it. This is a fate which Goethe shares with all who are great and important. If we would judge and use his utterances rightly, we must ask ourselves first of all: "When did these conversations take place, and to whom did Goethe talk?"

When? At a time when Goethe, in his old age, had turned away from art and applied all his intellectual energy to science; when also, bored by the insipid productions of younger writers, he was repelled by the loud and aggressive in literature.

To whom he talked? To a young man whom he wished to educate for his sake, as well as for his own purposes, and in whom he perhaps discovered more talent for quiet adaptation to others than for striking original productiveness. We see this illustrated in Goethe's warning to Eckermann, not to attempt ambitious literary tasks—a failing to

which we are all prone, and by which we harm
ourselves without benefiting literature.   It must,
however, be said that a literary epoch without the
ambition to produce something great, both as to
subject and form, would soon become insipid.
That ambition ought to exist even if the productive
ability be but moderate.   There is all the difference in the world between the requirements of the
old observer living in quiet retirement, and the
world of young talent, eternally rejuvenated and
carried away by the stream of life.

GRILLPARZER ON GOETHE AND SCHILLER

1836

In the supplement of the *Allgemeine Zeitung*
there appeared recently an article by an impartial
writer—whatever his name—who asserted that
real poetry was foreign to the German nature.   I
can imagine the great outcry against this in our
dear fatherland, unless, indeed, it is to be passed
over with supreme contempt.   Some will say:
"It is all wrong; Schiller may not be a stupendous
poet, but take Goethe, Goethe!"   But then I hear
others exclaim: "It may be admitted that Goethe
was not a real poet, but there is magnificent Schiller, in all the vigour of his German nature!"   Here
we see in anticipation all Germany divided into
two parties, each one of which asserts that one of

the two greatest representatives of German poetry
is not a real poet. This seems all the more peculiar inasmuch as every Greek believes firmly in
the greatness of Homer, and every Italian in Dante
and Ariosto, just as every Englishman, at least at
the present day, believes in the supreme greatness
of Shakespeare. From all this follows at least
clearly that the two greatest German poets did not
bear the true poetic stamp so unmistakably that
only dunces (and that neither of the two parties to
the quarrel can be called) could doubt its genuine-
ness. The truth seems to be that each of these
two great men lacked a certain poetic ingredient,
and that, according to their point of view, both
parties considered this ingredient precisely as the
most important element of poetry. And this is
exactly what the author of the article intended to
say.

SAINTE-BEUVE ON GOETHE

I

If I, as critic, may be permitted to invoke the example of the greatest of all critics, of Goethe, who
not only, as one may say, represents tradition, but
who unites in himself all traditions—which of
them, speaking of literature, predominates in him?
The classic element, is the answer. I see in his
works the temples of Greece, even as to the shores

CHARLES-AUGUSTIN SAINTE-BEUVE

of Tauris. He wrote *Werther*, but it is *Werther*
written by one who takes his Homer with him into
the fields, and who will find it again after his hero
has lost it. It is in this way that he has preserved
his supreme serenity. No one lives less in the
clouds than he; Parnassus grows in his hands; he
adds, as it were, new stairs to it, and there are
people in it at every halting place, at every summit, at every rocky projection. Possibly he makes
it resemble too much Montserrat, in Catalonia
(that mountain jagged rather than rounded); he
changes Parnassus, but does not destroy it.
Without his fondness for Greece, which counter-
acts his indifference or, if one prefers the word,
his universal curiosity, Goethe might have lost
himself in vagueness and infinity. If Olympus
had not been his favourite summit, where would he
have landed, among all the heights with which
he was familiar? Whither would he not have
roamed, he, the frankest of men, who, more than
any other, inclined toward the East? There would
have been no end to his transformations, his wan-
derings in pursuit of all the varied shapes of
beauty. But he always returns and rests; he
knows from what point of view the universe appears to the gaze in its most beautiful light; and
when we look for the embodiment of the highest
spirit of criticism, and its most comprehensive

thought, we think of him, an attentive and vigilant
spectator, watching from a distance, looking out
for new discoveries, noticing everything that
passes, spying for every sail on the horizon, but
looking down upon all this from the height of a
Sunium.—*Causeries du Lundi,* Vol. XV, "De la
Tradition en Littérature."

II

Let us lay aside for a moment our French habits
and try to form a just idea of Goethe. No one
has spoken better of Voltaire than he, no one has
understood and defined him better, as the highest
type of French genius; let us, in turn, render him
a like service by trying to understand him who was
the highest type of German genius. Goethe was,
with Cuvier, the last great man whom the century has lost. Goethe's chief characteristic was
breadth, indeed one may say universality. A
great naturalist and poet, he studies every object
and sees it at the same time in the world of reality
and in that of ideals; he studies its individual
characteristics and assigns to it its proper place
in the general order of nature. Meantime he extracts from it the poetic perfume which is inherent
in everything. Goethe drew poetry from everything; he was interested in everything. There
was not a human being, not a branch of study that

did not excite his curiosity. He was not satisfied
until he had grasped the smallest detail. One
might have said this was an all-absorbing passion;
but as soon as he had mastered one subject, he
turned aside and passed on to another. In his
noble mansion, which showed as a frontispiece the
word: *Salve,* he received strangers hospitably and
without discrimination,—talking with them in their
own language, bringing before them subjects with
which study had made them familiar, and pursu-
ing—serenely, calmly, without envy or bitterness
—no other aim than to *widen his own horizon.*
If any subject or any human being displeased
him, his interest ceased; he turned aside and cast
his glance at something else in that vast universe,
where he had merely to choose. Not that he had
become indifferent, he was merely no longer interested. But where his interest was active, he
was persistent—without being stirred at bottom.
He was benevolent as we imagine the gods to be,
truly Olympic—a word which on the other side
of the Rhine causes no smile. If there appeared
a new poet, a talent of marked originality, a
Byron, a Manzoni, Goethe forthwith began to
study him with extreme interest, and without any
merely personal and extraneous sentiment; he
had the *love of genius.* Take Manzoni, for instance. He had known nothing of him when his

Conte de Carmagnola fell into his hands; he at once took up the work eagerly, and buried himself in its study. He discovered in it a thousand beauties, caught its very intention, and one day, through the periodical *Kunst und Alterthum,* where he spoke so many of his thoughts, he announced Manzoni to all Europe.—*Causeries du Lundi,* Vol. II, "Lettres de Goethe et de Bettina.

LOWELL ON GOETHE

I

What kind of culture Shakespeare had is uncertain; how much he had is disputed; that he had as much as he wanted, and of whatever kind he wanted, must be clear to whoever considers the question. Dr. Farmer has proved, in his entertaining essay, that he got everything at second-hand from translations, and that, where his translator blundered, he loyally blundered too. But Goethe, the man of widest acquirement in modern times, did precisely the same thing. In his character of poet he set as little store by useless learning as Shakespeare did. He learned to write hexameters, not from Homer, but from Voss, and Voss found them faulty; yet somehow *Hermann und Dorothea* is more readable than *Luise.* So far as all the classicism then attainable was concerned, Shakespeare got it as cheap as Goethe did, who always bought it ready-made. For such purposes of mere æsthetic nourishment Goethe always milked other minds,—if minds those ruminators and digesters of antiquity into asses' milk may be called. There were plenty of professors who were forever assiduously browsing in vales of Enna and on Pentelican slopes among the vestiges of antiquity, slowly secreting lacteous facts, and not one of them would have raised his head from that exquisite pasturage, though Pan had made music through his pipe of reeds. Did Goethe wish to work up a Greek theme? He drove out Herr Böttiger, for example, among that fodder delicious to him for its very dryness, that sapless Arcadia of scholiasts, let him graze, ruminate, and go through all other needful processes of the antiquarian organism, then got him quietly into a corner and milked him. The product, after standing long enough, mantled over with the rich Goethean cream, from which a butter could be churned, if not precisely classic, quite as good as the ancients could have made out of the same material. But who has ever read the *Achilleis*, correct in all *un*essential particulars as it probably is?—*Shakespeare Once More.*

II

That the general want of style in German authors is not wholly the fault of the language is shown by Heine (a man of mixed blood), who can be daintily light in German; that it is not altogether a matter of race, is clear from the graceful airiness of Erasmus and Reuchlin in Latin, and of the Baron Grimm in French. The sense of heaviness which creeps over the reader from so many German books is mainly due, we suspect, to the language, which seems well-nigh incapable of that aerial perspective so delightful in first-rate French, and even English writing. But there must also be in the national character an insensibility to proportion, a want of that instinctive discretion which we call tact. Nothing short of this will account for the perpetual groping of German imaginative literature after some foreign mould in which to cast its thought or feeling, now trying a Louis Quatorze pattern, then something supposed to be Shakespearian, and at last going back to ancient Greece, or even Persia. Goethe himself, limpidly perfect as are many of his shorter poems, often fails in giving artistic coherence to his longer works. Leaving deeper qualities wholly out of the question, *Wilhelm Meister* seems a mere aggregation of episodes if compared with such a masterpiece as *Paul and Virginia,* or even with a happy improvisation like the *Vicar of Wakefield*. The second part of

Faust, too, is rather a reflection of Goethe's own
changed view of life and man's relation to it, than
a harmonious completion of the original conception. Full of placid wisdom and exquisite poetry
it certainly is; but if we look at it as a poem, it
seems more as if the author had striven to get
in all he could, than to leave out all he might. We
cannot help asking what business have paper
money and political economy and geognosy here?
We confess that Thales and the Homunculus
weary us not a little, unless, indeed, a poem be
nothing, after all, but a prolonged conundrum.
Many of Schiller's lyrical poems, though the best
of them find no match in modern verse for rapid
energy, the very axles of language kindling with
swiftness, seem disproportionately long in parts,
and the thought too often has the life well-nigh
squeezed out of it in the seven-fold coils of diction, dappled though it be with splendid imagery.

In German sentiment, which runs over so easily
into sentimentalism, a foreigner cannot help being struck with a certain incongruousness. What
can be odder, for example, than the mixture of sensibility and sausages in some of Goethe's earlier
notes to Frau von Stein, unless, to be sure, the
publishing them? It would appear that Germans
were less sensitive to the ludicrous—and we are
far from saying that this may not have its com-

pensatory advantages—than either the English or the French. And what is the source of this sensibility, if it be not an instinctive perception of the incongruous and disproportionate? Among all races, the English has ever shown itself most keenly alive to the fear of making itself ridiculous; and among all, none has produced so many humourists, only one of them, indeed, so profound as Cervantes, yet all masters in their several ways. What English-speaking man, except Boswell, could have arrived at Weimar, as Goethe did, in that absurd *Werthermontirung?* And where, out of Germany, could he have found a reigning Grand-Duke to put his whole court into the same sentimental livery of blue and yellow, leather breeches, boots, and all, excepting only Herder, and that not on account of his clerical profession, but of his age? To be sure, it might be asked also where else in Europe was a prince to be met with capable of manly friendship with a man whose only decoration was his genius?—*Essay on Lessing.*

LOWELL ON CLASSIC AND MODERN FORMS IN GERMAN LITERATURE

The first sincerely popular yearning toward antiquity, the first germ of Schiller's *Götter Griechenland's* is to be found in the old poem of Tannhäuser, very nearly coincident with the beginnings of the Reformation. And if we might allegorise it, we should say that it typified precisely that longing after Venus, under her other name of Charis, which represents the relation in which modern should stand to ancient art. It is the virile grace of the Greeks, their sense of proportion, their distaste for the exaggerated, their exquisite propriety of phrase, which steadies imagination without cramping it,—it is these that we should endeavour to assimilate without the loss of our own individuality. We should quicken our sense of form by intelligent sympathy with theirs, and not stiffen it into formalism by a servile surrender of what is genuine in us to what *was* genuine in them. "A pure form," says Schiller, "helps and sustains, an impure one hinders and shatters." But we should remember that the spirit of the age must enter as a modifying principle, not only into ideas, but into the best manner of their expression. The old bottles will not always serve for the new wine. A principle of iife is the first requirement of all art, and it can only be communicated by the touch of the time and a simple faith in it; all else is circumstantial and secondary. The Greek tragedy passed through the three natural stages of poetry,—the imaginative in Æschylus, the thoughtfully artistic in Sophocles, the sentimental in Euripides,—and then died. If people could only learn the general applicability to periods and schools of what young Mozart says of Gellert, that "he had written no poetry *since* his death"! No effort to raise a defunct past has ever led to anything but just enough galvanic twitching of the limbs to remind us unpleasantly of life. The romantic movement of the school of German poets which succeeded Goethe and Schiller ended in extravagant unreality, and Goethe himself, with his unerring common-sense, has given us, in the second part of *Faust,* the result of his own and Schiller's common striving after a Grecian ideal. Euphorion, the child of Faust and Helen, falls dead at their feet; and Helen herself soon follows him to the shades, leaving only her mantle in the hands of her lover. This, he is told, shall lift him above the earth. We fancy we can interpret the symbol. Whether we can or not, it is certainly suggestive of thought that the only immortal production of the greatest of recent poets was conceived and carried out in that Gothic spirit and form from which he was all his life struggling to break loose.—*Swinburne's Tragedies.*

ITALIAN LITERATURE

GOETHE ON DANTE

In recognising the qualities of Dante's great mind
and heart, we shall gain the proper appreciation
of his works if we keep in view the fact that just
at his time, which was also the time of Giotto,
plastic art reappeared in its natural strength.
The genius of the time, appealing powerfully to
the senses, dominated him also. His imagination
saw his subjects so clearly that he could easily
reproduce them in sharp outline; we therefore see
in him before us what is most strange and abstruse, as if drawn from Nature. He is never
hampered by the *terza rima;* on the contrary, it
assists him in carrying out his intention and
giving a sharp outline to his characters. . . .

The entire plan of the locality of Dante's *Inferno* has something minutely great (Mikromeg-
isches) about it and is therefore bewildering to
the senses. From above, down to the lowest
abyss, we must imagine circle within circle. This
gives us from the start the idea of an amphithea-
tre, which, however enormous it may be, always

appeals to our imagination as something limited by art, inasmuch as we can overlook from above everything, including the arena itself. If we look at Orcagna's picture, we seem to see before us an inverted cone instead of a funnel. The painter's idea is rhetorical rather than poetic, he arouses our imagination, but does not satisfy it.

But though unwilling to praise the *Inferno* as a whole, we are astonished by the strange profusion of individual localities—astonished, confused, and compelled to admire.—*Letter to Zelter,* September 6, 1826.

GRILLPARZER ON DANTE

1823

Nothing is more distasteful to me than far-fetched explanations of poetic works. A good poet is always able to express what he wishes to say; and what he intentionally conceals should not be forcibly dragged to the light, least of all be placed in the foreground as the principal thing. In the form of the thought lies the very essence of poetry. The thought, it is true, transcends the form, but what is nearest and most natural appears to us as the real truth. I apply all this even to Dante, whose *Inferno* delights me, as it does the whole world, but whose *Purgatorio,* and especially whose *Paradiso,* have always bored me.

Everything in it is supposed to be allegory,

while most of it is only imagery. The whole is a vision, in which what we see is supposed to be reality. Neither the apparitions in Hell nor those in Purgatory or Heaven ought to make us imagine anything different from what Dante tells us. Virgil is the shadow of the real poet Virgil—Dante's model and exemplar—with possibly, according to popular belief, a slight admixture of the magician; Beatrice is the real Beatrice, only, since she died at the age of nine, grown in purity and piety, so that she may be considered a paragon of all virtue.

Even the animals at the beginning, when the whole expresses a scene of roving, are just wild animals, such as the wanderer may meet with in a lonely wood. Nothing is said of them that is not in keeping with the real character of animals, and if we were to think of them in a different light, adding or omitting something, the imagery of the whole would be destroyed. That Dante himself had something different in mind admits scarcely of doubt, but the mere fact that we do not know what, deprives the allegory of all point.

———

1845

It is curious indeed that Dante's similes were

never taken from inanimate things, but always from human actions and conditions.

1846

Dante's great cradle song, with which he lulled to sleep his own passions and the sense of his unhappiness.—In his Hell we find his hatred, in his Purgatory his longing and in his Paradise his resignation. What is metaphysical and incorporeal in his Paradise expresses symbolically that there was no other consolation left to him than his studies, chief among which, according to the vision of the day, was scholastic theology.

SAINTE-BEUVE ON DANTE

Just as a little philosophy and science, as has been said, estranges us from religion, while much philosophy brings us back to it, so there is a degree of poetry which takes us away from history and reality, while a higher degree brings us back to them and, indeed, includes them. Dante's poem is the expression of the history of his time, as seen from the widest point of view—the expression not only of passions, of political hatreds and struggles, but also of the science, the beliefs, and the imaginings of those days. What Vico had ingeniously said of Dante, considered by him as a sort of ideal historian, has been strictly verified and confirmed by critical study and a careful examination of all the facts.

It is nevertheless certain that the original and principal inspiration of the *Divine Comedy* is a purely personal and, if one may say so, a lyrical inspiration. Having been in love, at the age of nine, with Beatrice, who was only eight, Dante kept up throughout his life that inconceivable cult of his affection, which would seem wholly fictitious were it not in accord with those subtle ideas characteristic of the age of chivalry. That love, whose principal incidents and adventures were limited to a few salutations, a few glances exchanged and a few smiles returned, at the utmost to a few rare words, and which never prevented either of the two persons who thus amused themselves from entering sooner or later into a marriage contract with some one else—that love which, moreover, seems to have been forever broken by the premature death of Beatrice at the age of twenty-six years, became and continued to be Dante's deep and predominating thought, and the noblest impulse of his conduct and his undertakings. It became his star and remained the symbol or, to speak more exactly, the essence and the flame of his highest virtue. Whenever he was about to commit any act which seemed to detract from this sentiment he was quickly filled with remorse; he secretly blushed before himself, and wished to atone for his fault. After having sung of his childish love in delicate and subtle verse, he felt that this was not enough, and that he ought to rear to the beauty who reigned in his heart an everlasting monument. Of this thought was born the *Divine Comedy,* and he spent years in constructing it, delving and toiling, raising his work in every sense and introducing into it whatever could give it life and beauty in the eyes of his contemporaries, so as to render more luminous and resplendent the throne on which he wished to place Beatrice before all the world.—*Causeries du Lundi,* Vol. XI, "La Divine Comédie."

LOWELL ON DANTE

I

It is not without significance that Goethe, who, like Dante, also absorbed and represented the tendency and spirit of his age, should, during his youth and while Europe was alive with the moral and intellectual longing which precluded the French Revolution, have loved the Gothic architecture. It is no less significant that in the period of reaction toward more positive thought which followed, he should have preferred Greek. His

greatest poem, conceived during the former era, is
Gothic. Dante, endeavouring to conform himself
to literary tradition, began to write the *Divina
Commedia* in Latin, and had elaborated several
cantos of it in that dead and intractable material.
But that poetic instinct, which is never the instinct
of an individual, but of his age, could not so be
satisfied, and leaving the classic structure he had
begun to stand as a monument of failure, he completed his work in Italian. Instead of endeavouring to manufacture a great poem out of what was
foreign and artificial, he let the poem make itself
out of him. The epic which he wished to write
in the universal language of scholars, and which
might have had its ten lines in the history of literature, would sing itself in provincial Tuscan, and
turns out to be written in the universal dialect of
mankind. Thus all great poets have been in a
certain sense provincial,—Homer, Dante, Shakespeare, Goethe, Burns, Scott in the *Heart of Mid-
lothian* and *Bride of Lammermoor*,—because the
office of the poet is always vicarious, because nothing that has not been living experience can become
living expression, because the collective thought,
the faith, the desire of a nation or a race, is the
cumulative result of many ages, is something organic, and is wiser and stronger than any single
person, and will make a great statesman or a

great poet out of any man who can entirely surrender himself to it.

As the Gothic cathedral, then, is the type of the Christian idea, so is it also of Dante's poem. And as that in its artistic unity is but the completed thought of a single architect, which yet could never have been realised except out of the faith and by the contributions of an entire people, whose beliefs and superstitions, whose imagination and fancy, find expression in its statues and its carvings, its calm saints and martyrs now at rest forever in the seclusion of their canopied niches, and its wanton grotesques thrusting themselves forth from every pinnacle and gargoyle, so in Dante's poem, while it is as personal and peculiar as if it were his private journal and autobiography, we can yet read the diary and the autobiography of the thirteenth century and of the Italian people. Complete and harmonious in design as his work is, it is yet no Pagan temple enshrining a type of the human made divine by triumph of corporeal beauty; it is not a private chapel housing a single saint and dedicated to one chosen bloom of Christian piety or devotion; it is truly a cathedral, over whose high altar hangs the emblem of suffering, of the Divine made human to teach the beauty of adversity, the eternal presence of the spiritual, not overhanging and threatening,

but informing and sustaining the material. In
this cathedral of Dante's there are side-chapels
as is fit, with altars to all Christian virtues and
perfections; but the great impression of its leading thought is that of aspiration, for ever and
ever. In the three divisions of the poem we may
trace something more than a fancied analogy with
a Christian basilica. There is first the ethnic
forecourt, then the purgatorial middle space, and
last the holy of holies dedicated to the eternal
presence of the mediatorial God.

II

Like all great artistic minds, Dante was essentially conservative, and, arriving precisely in that
period of transition when Church and Empire
were entering upon the modern epoch of thought,
he strove to preserve both by presenting the theory of both in a pristine and ideal perfection.
The whole nature of Dante was one of intense belief. There is proof upon proof that he believed
himself invested with a divine mission. Like the
Hebrew prophets, with whose writings his whole
soul was imbued, it was back to the old worship
and the God of the fathers that he called his people; and not Isaiah himself was more destitute of
that humour, that sense of ludicrous contrast,
which is an essential in the composition of a scep-

tic. In Dante's time, learning had something of a sacred character; the line was hardly yet drawn between the clerk and the possessor of supernatural powers; it was with the next generation, with the elegant Petrarch, even more truly than with the kindly Boccaccio, that the purely literary life, and that dilettantism, which is the twin sister of scepticism, began. As a merely literary figure, the position of Dante is remarkable. Not only as respects thought, but as respects æsthetics also, his great poem stands as a monument on the boundary line between the ancient and modern. He not only marks, but is in himself, the transition. *Arma virumque cano,* that is the motto of classic song; the things of this world and great men. Dante says, *subjectum est homo,* not *vir;* my theme is man, not a man. The scene of the old epic and drama was in this world, and its catastrophe here; Dante lays his scene in the human soul, and his fifth act in the other world. He makes himself the protagonist of his own drama. In the *Commedia* for the first time Christianity wholly revolutionises Art, and becomes its seminal principle. But æsthetically also, as well as morally, Dante stands between the old and the new, and reconciles them. The theme of his poem is purely subjective, modern, what is called romantic; but its treatment is objective (almost to realism, here and there), and it is limited by a form of classic severity. In the same way he sums up in himself the two schools of modern poetry which had preceded him, and, while essentially lyrical in his subject, is epic in the handling of it. So also he combines the deeper and more abstract religious sentiment of the Teutonic races with the scientific precision and absolute systematism of the Romanic. In one respect Dante stands alone. While we can in some sort account for such representative men as Voltaire and Goethe (nay, even Shakespeare) by the intellectual and moral fermentation of the age in which they lived, Dante seems morally isolated and to have drawn his inspiration almost wholly from his own internal reserves. Of his mastery in style we need say little here. Of his mere language, nothing could be better than the expression of Rivarol: "His verse holds itself erect by the mere force of the substantive and verb, without the help of a single epithet." We will only add a word on what seems to us an extraordinary misapprehension of Coleridge, who disparages Dante by comparing his Lucifer with Milton's Satan. He seems to have forgotten that the precise measurements of Dante were not prosaic, but absolutely demanded by the nature of his poem. He is describing an actual journey, and his exactness makes a part of the

verisimilitude. We read the *Paradise Lost* as a
poem, the *Commedia* as a record of fact; and no
one can read Dante without believing his story,
for it is plain that he believed it himself. It is
false æsthetics to confound the grandiose with the
imaginative. Milton's angels are not to be compared with Dante's, at once real and supernatural;
and the Deity of Milton is a Calvinistic Zeus, while
nothing in all poetry approaches the imaginative
grandeur of Dante's vision of God at the conclusion of the *Paradiso*. In all literary history there
is no such figure as Dante, no such homogeneous-
ness of life and works, such loyalty to ideas, such
sublime irrecognition of the unessential; and
there is no moral more touching than that the contemporary recognition of such a nature, so endowed and so faithful to its endowment, should
be summed up in the sentence of Florence: *Igne
comburatur sic quod moriatur.*

III

The relation of Dante to literature is monumen-
tal, and marks the era at which the modern begins.
He is not only the first great poet, but the first
great prose writer who used a language not yet
subdued to literature, who used it moreover for
scientific and metaphysical discussion, thus giving
an incalculable impulse to the culture of his coun-

trymen by making the laity free of what had hitherto been the exclusive guild of clerks. Whatever
poetry had preceded him, whether in the Romance
or Teutonic tongues, is interesting mainly for its
simplicity without forethought, or, as in the *Nibelungen,* for a kind of savage grandeur that rouses
the sympathy of whatever of the natural man is
dormant in us. But it shows no trace of the creative faculty either in unity of purpose or style,
the proper characteristics of literature. If it
have the charm of wanting artifice, it has not the
higher charm of art. We are in the realm of
chaos and chance, nebular, with phosphorescent
gleams here and there, star-stuff, but uncondensed
in stars. The *Nibelungen* is not without far-
reaching hints and forebodings of something finer
than we find in it, but they are a glamour from
the vague darkness which encircles it, like the
whisper of the sea upon an unknown shore at
night, powerful only over the more vulgar side of
the imagination, and leaving no thought, scarce
even any image (at least of beauty) behind them.
Such poems are the amours, not the lasting friend-
ships and possessions of the mind. They thrill
and cannot satisfy.

But Dante is not merely the founder of modern
literature. He would have been that if he had
never written anything more than his *Canzoni,*

which for elegance, variety of rhythm, and fervour of sentiment were something altogether new. They are of a higher mood than any other poems of the same style in their own language, or indeed in any other.   In beauty of phrase and subtlety of analogy they remind one of some of the Greek tragic choruses.—*Essay on Dante.*

SPANISH LITERATURE

GOETHE ON CALDERON

THE great point is that he from whom we would learn should be congenial to us. Thus, Calderon, for example, great as he is, and much as I admire him, has not influenced me in the least, either for good or ill. To Schiller indeed he might have become dangerous, as he would have led him astray. Therefore it is fortunate that Calderon was not generally appreciated in Germany until after Schiller's death. Calderon is infinitely great as regards technique and theatrical effect; Schiller's aims, on the other hand, were far higher and more serious. It would have been a pity indeed if those merits had been impaired without his attaining to the greatness of Calderon in other respects.—*Eckermann's Conversations with Goethe.*

GRILLPARZER ON CALDERON

1819

The curious direction which the latest æsthetic taste in Germany is taking admits of a very simple explanation; there is a concurrence of two factors: knowledge—historical, even scientific and analytical—of what was excellent in art before our days combined with actual impotence. The leaders in these æsthetic movements are what Jean Paul used to call feminine geniuses. They do not lack either receptivity or love for the beautiful, but they have not the power to give it form and create something living. Since, however, no one easily admits his own weakness, they do not look into their own hearts for the cause of their failure, but ascribe it to the absence of certain external conditions which they imagine existed before, but are no longer effective. Religion, they think, was responsible for the dramatic master-works of the Greeks and Spaniards, and since no one has religion nowadays, therefore no masterpieces are being produced. And all this leads to the prevailing hankering for what is called romanticism, to that longing, those presentiments and supernatural visions, for which there is no counterpart in nature anywhere. The great masters of all times, from Shakespeare and Milton to Goethe, were more or less plastic, because sharply defined plastic and individual creation,—the most difficult thing in art —is reserved only for the powerful master and is the aim of all his endeavour. Formlessness, which is the principal ingredient of so-called romanticism, has been from time immemorial the mark of a weak and sickly mind, unable to control itself and to attain the object of its efforts.

There are no ways of pigeon-holing and registering the many manifestations of the human intellect, as though they were a collection of insects. Metaphysical and religious ideas are changeable, but the essence of beauty is immutable. Subjective truths remain, even if the objective truth of our dreams has long been lost; and sentiments which have always existed and, according to an inexplicable law of human nature, always will exist, are, in spite of their vagueness, more useful for the purposes of poetic art than the so-called truths stored up as unapproachable canons of a philosophic or religious system. Let us look at Calderon. A hundred times he has made use of Catholic superstition (which is nothing but masked pagan, or, to call it by its right name, human superstition), but hardly once has he made religious faith his subject. And yet this very superstition moves profoundly, in poetry, men who despise it in religion.

1820

It is curious to see with what gallantry Calderon's knights treat their ladies as long as their mutual relations are merely those of lovers, and how indifferent the poet becomes towards them when the question of marriage is at issue. His female characters are, as a rule, finally disposed of in some fashion; any husband is good enough for them—even a man whom they formerly rejected, or who rejected them. But such is the essence of gallantry; almost unknown to the ancients, it owed its origin only to the fact that Christianity so severely frowned down upon the crowning favour which is the real object of love. It may be imagined how gentle and tender the struggle between desire and renunciation would make those sturdy knights, particularly in the Southern countries. As a matter of fact, gallantry appeared first in Spain and in southern France. It spread to Germany only with the introduction of Provençal poetry, and really remained in that country always an exotic product. There is not a trace of it in the Nibelungenlied. Altogether, the peculiarities of romantic poetry may be explained by the inversion of the relations between body and soul due to the teachings of Christianity, which rejected the demands of the body as sinful, and thereby planted the seeds of an eternal struggle—a struggle which led to all those melancholy broodings that are the bane of modern times. When shall there ever be found a *medius terminus?*

1838

In the narratives and the sermonising which occur in Calderon's plays dialectic expressions are not only tolerated, but are especially emphasised or imitated by the poet, as possessing a beauty of their own.

1851

It seems curious that in the collection of eulogistic poems in honour of Lope de Vega, which Montalvan published after his death, Calderon is not represented, which seems to point to the existence of a decided enmity between the two dramatists. At any rate, the unbounded and exclusive praise of Lope de Vega in these poems carries with it a certain sting against his rival, who, if less favoured by nature, attained beyond a doubt a greater maturity.

LOWELL ON CALDERON

Since Virgil there have been at most but four cosmopolitan authors,—Dante, Cervantes, Shakespeare, and Goethe. These have stood the supreme test of being translated into all tongues, because the large humanity of their theme, and of their handling of it, needed translation into none. Calderon is a greater poet than Goethe, but even in the most masterly translation he retains still a Spanish accent, and is accordingly *interned* (if I may Anglicise a French word) in that provincialism which we call nationality.— *Address on Wordsworth.*

GRILLPARZER ON LOPE DE VEGA

1837

Shakespeare has often something symbolical in his manner of depicting sentiment and passion; he gives us the metaphysics of passion, a *précis* and *abrégé* of sentiment. What Lope de Vega depicts is pure nature.

———

If Calderon is the Schiller of Spanish literature, Lope de Vega is its Goethe.

———

Calderon has the grand manner, Lope paints nature itself.

———

Schiller and Calderon seem to be philosophical writers, Goethe and Lope de Vega are such in fact. Schiller and Calderon give us philosophical discussions, Goethe and Lope de Vega show us the results.

1839

Lope fared very badly in the judgment of foreign nations. All that people know of him is that

he was a man of extraordinary fertility, that he
wrote some three thousand comedies, and composed each day of his life perhaps two or three
hundred verses. Lord Holland has recently published a book about him, and A. W. Schlegel has
mentioned him in his lectures on dramatic art.
Lord Holland compares him with Cervantes, that
is to say, he makes poor Lope appear as a sort of
half-crazy genius, a scribbler who, with all his
gifts, made a failure of his profession, and who
ranks far below his famous countryman and contemporary. And in reality, if one compares the
immortal *Don Quixote* with any single work of
Lope's, it seems as if we compared a sage and a
school-boy. In reality the comparison is quite
unjust. All the works of Cervantes that have
come down to us, good as they are in part, do not
add one iota to the impression *Don Quixote* produces upon us or to our admiration for its author;
while we do not know Lope de Vega at all if we
have read merely a dozen of his plays, even of his
best. The more we read of him, the more we wonder at the wealth of his poetic genius, until we
are forced to conclude that, granting all his
defects and all his carelessness, he has not his
equal in truth to nature, artistic feeling, variety, and power to give reality to his concep-
tions.

GRILLPARZER ON THE CONTRAST BETWEEN SPANISH AND GERMAN DRAMATISTS

1839

The great difference between the dramatic poetry of the Spaniards and the Germans lies mainly in the national differences of character. The German is tender and sentimental. He would imbue life with poetry and enjoy its fancied reality. Therefore he is more interested in how a drama ends than in how its plot is developed; for it is the end that gives the play its real value. To the Spaniard, however, the drama is a play, pure and simple. He follows the plot with sympathy and admiration, but when his interest has been aroused to the highest pitch, and he is, as it were, in the thick of the action, with all his heart and soul, he enjoys being disillusioned by an abrupt ending, which restores him to his normal self. Even Calderon, who is in other respects more consistent, allows the characters in his plays, before the curtain is finally lowered, to address the audience and to destroy all illusion by invoking their indulgence ("perdonen sus muchas faltas"). The German regards poesy as a mansion in which he would wish to dwell; the Spaniard as a garden in which he saunters at pleasure. The former seems more poetical, the latter is such in fact.

GRILLPARZER ON CERVANTES
1842

In the second part of *Don Quixote,* at the beginning of Chapter 44, Cervantes explains why he inserted in the first part stories which bear no relation to the whole, such as the *Curioso Impertinente* and the *Capitan Cautivo.* He did it, he says, in order to relieve the monotony and dryness resulting from the uniform recital of the adventures of the hero and his squire. But so far was he from considering this procedure a virtue (as Tieck does) that he concluded to abstain from it in the second part. And he was right, for what he had done was inartistic. Poetic variety must be an organic part of the main action, as it is in *Wilhelm Meister,* but cannot be introduced piecemeal in fragmentary stories.

Altogether Tieck sees *Don Quixote,* like everything else, in a false light. What Cervantes's artistic wisdom allows only occasionally to emerge from the background: the originally noble nature and the lucid moments of his hero, all this Tieck would place in the foreground, thus making Don Quixote the martyr of chivalry instead of the fool he actually is. The author has exerted all his ingenuity in order to make his hero ridiculous and to entertain the reader; indeed Don

Quixote's folly would show still fewer lucid moments if Cervantes had not wished to air some of his own views through the mouth of his hero.

There is a remarkable passage in Lord Byron's *Don Juan* about *Don Quixote* which is worth mentioning in this connection. Byron dates from Cervantes's work the decay of the Spanish character, which from that time began to lose its chivalrous traits. There is more truth in this than in all of Ludwig Tieck's phrases about poetry and poets.

1843

There is a stage direction in Cervantes's *Casa de los Celos,* which seems to point to a curious arrangement of the old Spanish stage. Angelica arrives on horseback with her followers, and there is this remark: "ha de entrar por el patio" (she is to enter from the pit), while the persons on the stage notice her and talk about her. There is a further direction: "da una vuelta al patio," whereupon she is lifted from her horse and the emperor commands that she be received at the foot of the stairs. In the next scene there is a further direction: "entra en el teatro Angelica." It seems, therefore, that the pit, like the orchestra of the ancients, played a part in the dramatic performances.

All those eight comedies which Cervantes never

lived to see performed, and which he printed
shortly before his death, make a sad impression.
They were issued for the second time in 1749, and
the publisher thinks that he cannot honour the
memory of his author better than by reviling Lope
de Vega and Calderon as the destroyers of good
comedy (the fact being that they were rather the
fathers of Spanish comedy of whatever kind).
Cervantes, says the publisher, did not intend his
plays to be real comedies, but merely parodies of
the works of those destroyers of art. As a matter of fact, they really surpass in their inartistic
and grotesque form the works of those popular
playwrights; but it is easy to see that Cervantes
would have been only too willing to rival them in
popular esteem, if he had not been partly too sagacious, partly too little of a poet. He reluctantly
enters upon the contest with them, and does not
expect to be victorious. Possibly he was driven
to authorship by his straightened circumstances.
He could find no actor willing to appear in his
comedies, which are as absurd as those of his
rivals, without being as enjoyable or elevating.
Even the versification is often harsh and the
rhymes are forced.

Lope is often reproached, and not unjustly, with
the absurdity of the adventures and complications
in his plots; but when we read these comedies of

Cervantes, who certainly was not lacking in intelligence and judgment, and see how much more improbable and senseless are their plots and their treatment of it, we come to the conclusion that it was the taste of the public that forced their clear intellects to write such incongruous stuff. *La Casa de los Celos* is the most disconnected, pointless play that was ever written, and yet it is by the author of *Don Quixote*.

LOWELL ON CERVANTES

I

Cervantes is the father of the modern novel, in so far as it has become a study and delineation of character instead of being a narrative seeking to interest by situation and incident. He has also more or less directly given impulse and direction to all humouristic literature since his time. We see traces of him in Molière, in Swift, and still more clearly in Sterne and Richter. Fielding assimilated and Smollett copied him. Scott was his disciple in the *Antiquary*, that most delightful of his delightful novels. Irving imitated him in his *Knickerbocker*, and Dickens in his *Pickwick Papers*. I do not mention this as detracting from *their* originality, but only as showing the wonderful virility of *his*. The pedigrees of books are as interesting and instructive as those of men. It is also good for us to remember that this man whose life was outwardly a failure restored to Spain the universal empire she had lost.

II

If you wish to know what humour is, I should say read *Don Quixote*. It is the element in which the whole story lives and moves and has its being, and it wakens and flashes round the course of the narrative like a phosphorescent sea in the track of a ship. It is nowhere absent; it is nowhere obtrusive; it lightens and plays about the surface for a moment and is gone. It is everywhere by suggestion, it is nowhere with emphasis and insistence. There is infinite variety, yet always in harmony with the characters and the purpose of the fable. The impression it produces is cumulative, not sudden or startling. It is unobtrusive as the tone of good conversation. I am not speaking of the *fun* of the book, of which there is plenty, and sometimes boisterous enough, but of that deeper and more delicate quality, suggestive of remote analogies and essential incongruities, which alone deserves the name of humour.

III

I have called *Don Quixote* a cosmopolitan book, and I know of none other that can compete with

it in this respect unless it be *Robinson Crusoe.*
But *Don Quixote,* if less verisimilar as a narrative,
and I am not sure that it is, appeals to far higher
qualities of mind and demands a far subtler sense
of appreciation than the masterpiece of Defoe. If
the latter represent in simplest prose what interests us because it *might* happen to any man, the
other, while seeming never to leave the low level
of fact and possibility, constantly suggests the
loftier region of symbol, and sets before us that
eternal contrast between the ideal and the real, between the world as it might be and the world as
it is, between the fervid completeness of conception and the chill inadequacy of fulfilment, which
life sooner or later, directly or indirectly, forces
upon the consciousness of every man who is more
than a patent digester. There is a moral in *Don
Quixote,* and a very profound one, whether Cervantes consciously put it there or not, and it is
this: that whoever quarrels with the Nature of
Things, wittingly or unwittingly, is certain to get
the worst of it. The great difficulty lies in finding out what the Nature of Things really and per-
durably is, and the great wisdom, after we have
made this discovery, or persuaded ourselves that
we have made it, is in accommodating our lives
and actions to it as best we may or can. And yet,
though all this be true, there is another and deeper

moral in the book than this.   The pathos which underlies its seemingly farcical turmoil, the tears
which sometimes tremble under our lids after
its most poignant touches of humour, the
sympathy with its hero which survives all his
most ludicrous defeats and humiliations and
is only deepened by them, the feeling that
he is after all the one noble and heroic figure
in a world incapable of comprehending him, and to
whose inhabitants he is distorted and caricatured
by the crooked panes in those windows of custom
and convention through which they see him, all
this seems to hint that only he who has the
imagination to conceive and the courage to attempt
a trial of strength with what foists itself in our
senses as the Order of Nature for the time being,
can achieve great results or kindle the co-operative
and efficient enthusiasm of his fellowmen.   The
Don Quixote of one generation may live to hear
himself called the saviour of society by the next.
How exalted was Don Quixote's own conception of
his mission is clear from what is said of his first
sight of the inn, that "it was as if he had seen a
star which guided him not to the portals, but to
the fortress of his redemption," where the allusion
were too daring were he not persuaded that he is
going forth to redeem the world.   Cervantes, of
course, is not so much speaking·in his own person,

as telling what passed in the mind of his hero. But he would not have ventured such an allusion in jest.

IV

Spaniards have not been wanting who protested against what they consider to be the German fashion of interpreting their national author. Don Juan Valera, in particular, one of the best of contemporary Spanish men of letters, both as critic and novelist, has argued the negative side of the question with force and acumen in a discourse pronounced on his admission to the Spanish Academy. But I must confess that, while he interested, he did not convince me. I could quite understand his impatience at what he considered the supersubtleties of interpretation to which our Teutonic cousins, who have taught us so much, are certainly somewhat prone. We have felt it ourselves when the obvious meaning of Shakespeare has been rewritten into Hegelese, by some Doctor of Philosophy desperate with the task of saying something when everything had been already said, and eager to apply his new theory of fog as an illuminating medium. But I do not think that transcendental criticism can be charged with indiscretion in the case of *Don Quixote*. After reading all that can be said against the justice of its deductions, or

divinations if you choose to call them so, I am inclined to say, as Turner did to the lady who, after
looking at one of his pictures, declared that she
could not see all this in nature, "Madam, don't
you wish to heaven you could?" I believe that
in all really great imaginative work we are aware,
as in nature, of something far more deeply interfused with our consciousness, underlying the obvious and familiar, as the living spirit of them,
and accessible only to a heightened sense and a
more passionate sympathy. He reads most wisely
who thinks everything into a book that it is capable
of holding, and it is the stamp and token of a great
book so to incorporate itself with our own being,
so to quicken our insight and stimulate our
thought, as to make us feel as if we helped to
create it while we read. Whatever we can find in
a book that aids us in the conduct of life, or to a
truer interpretation of it, or to a franker reconcile-
ment with it, we may with a good conscience believe is not there by accident, but that the author
meant that we should find it there. Cervantes
certainly intended something of far wider scope
than a mere parody on the Romances of Chivalry,
which before his day had ceased to have any vitality as motives of human conduct, or even as pictures of a life that anybody believed to have ever
existed except in dreamland. That he *did* intend

his book as a good-humoured criticism on *doctri-naire* reformers who insist, in spite of all history and experience, on believing that society is a device of human wit or an imposture of human cunning, and not a growth, an evolution from natural causes, is clear enough in more than one passage to the thoughtful reader. It is also a satire on all attempts to remake the world by the means and methods of the past, and on the humanity of impulse which looks on each fact that rouses its pity or its sense of wrong as if it was or could be complete in itself, and were not indissolubly bound up with myriads of other facts both in the past and the present. When we say that we are all of us the result of the entire past, we perhaps are not paying the past a very high compliment; but it is no less true that whatever happens is in some sense, more or less strict, the result of all that has happened before. As with all men of heated imaginations, a near object of compassion occupies the whole mind of Don Quixote; the figure of the present sufferer looms gigantic and shuts out all perception of remoter and more general considerations. Don Quixote's quarrel is with the structure of society, and it is only by degrees, through much mistake and consequent suffering, that he finds out how strong that structure is; nay, how strong it must be in order that the world may go smoothly and the course of events not be broken by a series of cataclysms. The French Revolutionists with the sincerest good intentions set about reforming in Don Quixote's style, and France has been in commotion ever since. They carefully grubbed up every root that drew its sustenance from the past and have been finding out ever since to their sorrow that nothing with roots can be made to order. "Do right though the heavens fall" is an admirable precept so long as the heavens do not take you at your word and come down about your ears—still worse about those of your neighbours. It is a rule rather of private than public obligation—for indeed it is the doing of right that *keeps* the heavens from falling. After Don Quixote's temporary rescue of the boy Andrés from his master's beating, the manner in which he rides off and discharges his mind of consequences is especially characteristic of reform by theory without study of circumstances. It is a profound stroke of humour that the reformer Don Quixote should caution Sancho not to attempt making the world over again, and to adapt himself to things as he finds them.—*Essay on Don Quixote.*

THE ANCIENTS

GOETHE ON EURIPIDES

SHAKESPEARE and Calderon cannot be sufficiently praised, although I should not have been greatly astonished if Schlegel had tried to drag them also down into the mire. He is just to Æschylus and Sophocles, not because he seems impressed by their extraordinary merits, but because among philologists it has become the proper thing to rank them both very highly. As a matter of fact, Schlegel's own little self cannot comprehend, or sufficiently appreciate, such lofty natures. Were he able to do so, he would also have been just to Euripides, and treated him quite differently. But all he knows of Euripides is that the philologists do not regard him very highly, and it flatters him not a little that he, backed by great authorities, has the privilege of mercilessly attacking the great ancient writer and lecturing him on his mistakes. I do not deny that Euripides has his faults; but he was nevertheless a worthy competitor of Sophocles and Æschylus. If he lacked the high seriousness and the artistic perfection of his predecessors, and as a dramatic writer treated things a little more carelessly and more in accord with average human nature, he probably knew the Athenian public sufficiently to recognise that they responded to the chord struck by him. The poet whom Socrates called his friend, whom Aristotle praised so highly, whom Menander admired, and for whom Sophocles and the city of Athens put on mourning on hearing of his death, must have been a man of no mean calibre. If a modern man like Schlegel has to find fault with so great an ancient, he ought not to do it otherwise than upon his knees.—*Eckermann's Conversations with Goethe.*

GOETHE ON THE GREEK TRAGEDIANS

The decline of tragic art among the Greeks could no more have been brought about by Euripides than the decline of sculpture could have been caused by some great artist who lived in the time of Phidias but was less great than he. When the epoch is great, it follows in the path of excellence, and what is of less value has no influence. Euripides lived in a time of superlative greatness. It was not a period of retrograding, but of progressive, taste. The art of sculpture had not yet reached its highest summit, and painting was still in its infancy.

If the plays of Euripides, compared with those of Sophocles, had great faults, it does not follow that succeeding poets were bound to imitate these faults and thereby come to grief; but if the plays of Euripides had such great merits that some could prefer them even to the plays of Sophocles, why did not succeeding poets endeavour to imitate these merits, and why did they not become at least as great as Euripides himself?

As a matter of fact, after the three famous great tragedians there appeared no fourth or fifth or sixth poet of equal greatness, and it is not easy to account for this fact, although one may venture to have an opinion and thus approximate the truth.

Man is a simple being, however rich, varied, and unfathomable his inner life may be. The circumstances in which he lives and moves are narrowly bounded. Had conditions among the Greeks been as they are with us poor Germans, for whom Lessing wrote two or three, I myself three or four, and Schiller five or six, passable plays, there would have been room enough for a fourth, fifth, or sixth tragedian.

But with the wonderful productiveness of the Greeks, whose three great poets had written each a hundred, or nearly a hundred plays, and who had treated the tragic subjects of Homer and the Heroic Age, in part, three or four times—when we consider the tragic wealth already then existing, it is a reasonable assumption that the subjects

gradually became exhausted, so that a poet following the three greatest was at a loss for a fitting
theme.

And, indeed, why should more plays have been
written? Were there not enough for some time to
come? And were not the productions of Æschylus, Sophocles, and Euripides so great and profound that one could hear them again and again
without their becoming trivial and stale? Even
the few superb fragments that have come down
to us are of such weight and such importance that
we poor Europeans have been busy with them for
centuries and shall continue for centuries to feed
and feast on them.—*Eckermann's Conversations
with Goethe.*

GRILLPARZER ON EURIPIDES

1823

The prologues of Euripides have been censured
as being contrary to reason. We must, however,
bear in mind that the ancient tragedies dealt with
generally known facts. If it be asked, Why dwell
in the prologue on what is so well known? the answer is that, in spite of it, a few of the spectators
might possibly have been ignorant of the subject,
and that others were not sufficiently familiar with
it in all its details. Since it was impossible to
incite and deepen curiosity in the plot, curiosity

was ruled out from the very beginning, and the entire treatment of the subject was, as it were, reversed, knowledge of what was to happen in the end producing the same effect that ignorance of it would have done.

Thus in the scene where Hecuba learns that the shade of Achilles has demanded one of the Trojan women as an expiatory sacrifice, and asks the gods to avert death from her daughter, the spectator knows in advance that inevitable death is her portion. The action thus takes place merely among the persons of the play, without the participation of the spectator. Pity gains what is lost in fear, and tragic emotion remains pure.

Very characteristic is the hatred of Euripides towards Helen and her relatives. We see in it the predominance of the philosophical view over the mythical. This may not seem sufficiently poetic at a first glance, but it was the inevitable result of the progress of time and culture. Poetry uses belief gladly enough where it exists, but it cannot recreate what has been lost.

In the mouth of Hecuba the reference to Helen is admirable, and the entire speech a masterpiece. The cool, statesman-like and (according to the standards of the time) by no means harsh speech of Ulysses forms a beautiful dramatic contrast to Hecuba's passionate words. We see in it the contrast between Barbarism and Hellenism. There is a beauty in the speech of Polyxena with which nothing modern can be compared. Woe is me that I was born in an age that does not recognise this!

The *Alcestis* of Euripides has from the very beginning something revolting for modern taste. We cannot tolerate that Admetus clings to life at any cost, and in cowardly fashion accepts the death of his wife as a sacrifice for his own preservation —nay that, even after she has died, he blames his own aged father for not having died instead of her. But what is disgusting in his behaviour disappears largely if one reflects that after Alcestis had offered herself as a sacrifice for her husband, no retraction or change was possible, according to the religious notions of the Greek. All that Admetus could do was to die *with* his wife, but not *for* her. The powers below had accepted the expiatory sacrifice, and it remained irrevocable. When Admetus, in the presence of the corpse of his wife, reproaches his father for not having died for him—his son—he probably thinks, grief-stricken as he is, only of Alcestis and her sacrifice. He has only room for the thought that his wife, the wife who lies dead before him, might have been spared if the old man, tottering to his grave, had not loved life more than he did the son. The presence of the beloved body robs the accusations of the son of their unnaturalness. How beautiful is his subsequent behaviour, when he keeps from the returning Heracles the death of his wife, in order not to sadden his entrance into the house! How fine the scene where Heracles wishes to put Alcestis, whom he has wrested from Thanatos, disguised and unrecognisable, into Admetus's charge, and Admetus refuses to receive her, lest by merely being near a woman he offend the memory of his wife! What a magnificent figure is Heracles, powerful and full of the joy of living, ready to turn away from the house as soon as he hears that mourning and sorrow reign in it; giving himself up unconcernedly to loud rejoicing as long as he sees no good reason for what seems to him the exaggerated sorrow of his host, but quickly resuming his dignity and ready to repay Admetus's nobility in fitting fashion as soon as he learns the connection of the whole. The scene where all is unravelled might have been written by Calderon, so thoroughly romantic is it. The rest, it is true, is decidedly Greek, but then we are dealing with a Greek tragedy.

Schlegel criticises very unjustly the *Orestes* of Euripides. His view seems to me wholly errone-

ous. The tragedies of the ancients cannot at all
be compared with our drama; at the utmost they
resemble the *autos sacramentales* of the Spaniards. Human actions are in most of them merely
an incident, or rather only the vehicle which con-
veys the real contents of the play—the glory or the
justification of the hero, the doings of the gods,
the force of fate. Strictly speaking, the *Œdipus
Tyrannus* is the only ancient tragedy in a modern
sense. Aristotle, who came much later has, in
spite of his keen (though prosaic) intellect, entirely overlooked the salient characteristics of the
tragedy and merely analysed the sub-stratum,
without entering into the deeper significance of
the essence. In this he was not so wrong, considering his position as teacher of science and of art.

Orestes was only created to give voice to the indignation of the Greeks against Helen evoked by
the Persian wars, long after Homer's superb descriptions had passed out of popular memory.
The murder of Helen, which seems so atrocious to
Schlegel, was perhaps precisely what delighted
the Athenians, and I can imagine the applause
evoked by that admirable chorus scene during the
deed and by the apparition and narrative of the
Phrygian. Such at least was the meaning of it all.

Orestes is evidently, as Schlegel assumes, the

middle part of a connected trilogy; otherwise how
could Apollo predict that Orestes would be declared guiltless in the Areopagus—a prediction
which would naturally deprive the concluding play
of all its interest.

Schlegel censures severely the scene where Py-
lades and Orestes declare their resolve to kill
Helen, and yet this very scene is unutterably magnificent. I can imagine the two, as they half whisper to each other in rapid discourse, with an
almost frenzied joy, what they have planned. Unconsciously they are drawn into the irresistible
whirlpool of fate, the fate of the children of Tan-
talus, θανάτους θανάτων ἀμοιβάς, which is finally so
gloriously averted by the intervention of Apollo,
who puts an end to the awful duty of retaliatory
murder.

The Greeks show in everything a quiet development, a comfortable enjoyment, as it were, of
detailed description, which we moderns find almost offensive, particularly in the drama. This
trait runs through the whole of their literature.
Their life was full of incident, but their enjoyment was placid; with us life is placid, therefore we relish so greatly variety and rapid
change.

GRILLPARZER ON THE GREEK CHORUS
1841

There is in the tragedies of Æschylus, and even in those of his successors, something awkward, a certain immovableness, which the moderns, accustomed to the rapid development of the plot, cannot tolerate. Indeed, the tragedies of Æschylus may, as has been done, be called dramatised epics. We have the situation and the declamation. The continuance of the action is often marked by a single event, a mere incident, as compared with the broad description of conditions and opinions. The chorus, whatever may be said about it, revolves around the same observations and the same moral. In the antiphonies the discourse requires endless time before the persons come to an understanding about the simplest things; what the spectator has understood from the first reply is asked again and again through ten verses, until an agreement is reached. It is something of the awkwardness which shows itself at the present day in our folk-songs, and is characteristic of a certain idle enjoyment, such as children and simple-minded people betray in listening again and again to a story which they have heard ten times before, and know by heart from beginning to end.

Later on we find in Euripides, as we have already found in Sophocles, that kind of talkativeness which the Athenians had learned to relish in their public discourses and their judicial trials. This talkativeness, in the better sense of the word, is not even rare in Plato's Dialogues.

LOWELL ON THE GREEKS

Only those languages can properly be called dead in which nothing living has been written. If the classic languages are dead, they yet speak to us, and with a clearer voice than that of any living tongue.

> "Graiis ingenium, Graiis dedit ore rotundo
> Musa loqui, praeter laudem nullius avaris."

If their language is dead, yet the literature it enshrines is rammed with life as perhaps no other writing, except Shakespeare's, ever was or will be. It is as contemporary with to-day as with the ears it first enraptured, for it appeals not to the man of then or now, but to the entire round of human nature itself. Men are ephemeral or evanescent, but whatever page the authentic soul of man has touched with her immortalising finger, no matter how long ago, is still young and fair as it was to the world's grey fathers. Oblivion looks in the face of the Grecian Muse only to forget her errand. Plato and Aristotle are not names but things. On a chart that should represent the firm earth and wavering oceans of the human mind, they would be marked as mountain-ranges, forever modifying the temperature, the currents, and the atmosphere of thought, astronomical stations whence the movements of the lamps of heaven might best be observed and predicted. Even for the mastering of our own tongue, there is no expedient so fruitful as translation out of another; how much more when that other is a language at once so precise and so flexible as the Greek! Greek literature is also the most fruitful comment on our own. Coleridge has told us with what profit he was made to study Shakespeare and Milton in conjunction with the Greek dramatists. It is no sentimental argument for this study that the most justly balanced, the most serene, and the most fecundating minds since the revival of learning have been steeped in and saturated with Greek literature. We know not whither other studies will lead us, especially if dissociated from this; we do not know to what summits, far above our lower region of turmoil, this has led, and what the many-sided outlook thence.—*Address at the Two Hundred and Fiftieth Anniversary of Harvard.*

LOWELL'S CONTRAST BETWEEN ANCIENTS AND MODERNS

A book may be great in other ways than as a les-

son in form, and it may be for other qualities that
it is most precious to us. Is it nothing, then, to
have conversed with genius? Goethe's *Iphigenie*
is far more perfect in form than his *Faust,* which
is indeed but a succession of scenes strung together on a thread of moral or dramatic purpose,
yet it is *Faust* that we read and hold dear alike
for its meaning and for the delight it gives
us. And if we talk of classics: what then is
a classic, if it be not a book that forever
delights, inspires, and surprises—in which and
in ourselves, by its help, we make new discoveries every day? What book has so warmly em-
bosomed itself in the mind and memory of men as
the Iliad? And yet surely not by its perfection in
form as much as by the stately simplicity of its
style, by its pathetic truth to nature, for so loose
and discursive is its plan as to have supplied plausible argument for a diversity of authorship.
What work of classic antiquity has given the
bransle, as he would have called it, to more fruitful thinking than the Essays of Montaigne, the
most planless of men who ever looked before and
after, a chaos indeed, but a chaos swarming with
germs of evolution? There have been men of
genius, like Emerson, richly seminative for other
minds; like Browning, full of wholesome ferment
for other minds, though wholly destitute of any

proper sense of form.—*The Study of Modern Languages.*

II

Shall we say that the literature of the last three centuries is incompetent to put a healthy strain upon the more strenuous faculties of the mind? That it does not appeal to and satisfy the mind's loftier desires? That Dante, Machiavelli, Montaigne, Bacon, Shakespeare, Cervantes, Pascal, Calderon, Lessing, and he of Weimar in whom Carlyle and so many others have found their University,—that none of these set our thinking gear in motion to as good purpose as any ancient of them all? Is it less instructive to study the growth of modern ideas than of ancient? Is the awakening of the modern world to consciousness and its first tentative, then fuller, then rapturous expression of it, like

—"The new-abashed nightingale
That stinteth first when she beginneth sing,"

"Till the fledged notes at length forsake their nests,
Fluttering in wanton shoals,"

less interesting or less instructive to us because it finds a readier way to our sympathy through a postern which we cannot help leaving sometimes on the latch, than through the ceremonious portal

of classical prescription?   Goethe went to the root
of the matter when he said, "people are always
talking of the study of the ancients; yet what
does this mean but apply yourself to the actual
world and seek to express it, since this is what the
ancients also did when they were alive?"   That
"when they were *alive*" has an unconscious sar-
casm in it.   I am not ashamed to confess that the
first stammerings of our English speech have a
pathetic charm for me which I miss in the wiser
and ampler utterances of a tongue, not only foreign to me as modern languages are foreign, but
thickened in its more delicate articulations by the
palsying touch of Time.   And from the native
wood-notes of many modern lands, from what it
was once the fashion to call the rude beginnings
of their literature, my fancy carries away, I think,
something as precious as Greek or Latin could
have made it.

III

In reading such books as chiefly deserve to be
read in any foreign language, it is wise to translate consciously and in words as we read.   There
is no such help to a fuller mastery of our vernac-
ular.   It compels us to such a choosing and test-
ing, to so nice a discrimination of sound, propriety,
position, and shade of meaning, that we now first

learn the secret of the words we have been using
or misusing all our lives, and are gradually made
aware that to set forth even the plainest matter,
as it should be set forth, is not only a very difficult
thing, calling for thought and practice, but an affair of conscience as well. Translating teaches us
as nothing else can, not only that there is a best
way, but that it is the only way. Those who have
tried it know too well how easy it is to grasp the
verbal meaning of a sentence or of a verse. That
is the bird in the hand. The real meaning, the
soul of it, that which makes it literature and not
jargon, *that* is the bird in the bush which tantalises
and stimulates with the vanishing glimpses we
catch of it as it flits from one to another lurking-
place,—

"Et fugit ad salices et se cupit ante videri."

After all, I am driven back to my Virgil again,
you see, for the happiest expression of what I was
trying to say. It was these shy allurements and
provocations of Omar Khayyám's Persian which
led Fitzgerald to many a peerless phrase and
made an original poet of him in the very act of
translating. I cite this instance merely by way
of hint that as a spur to the mind, as an open-ses-
ame to the treasures of our native vocabulary, the
study of a living language (for literary, not lingu-

istic, ends) may serve as well as that of any which
we rather inaptly call dead. . . .

IV

I cannot bring myself to look upon the literatures of the ancient and modern worlds as antagonists, but rather as friendly rivals in the effort
to tear as many as may be from the barbarising
plutolatry which seems to be so rapidly supplant-
ing the worship of what alone is lovely and endur-
ing. No, they are not antagonists, but by their
points of disparity, of likeness, or contrast, they
can be best understood, perhaps understood only
through each other. The scholar must have them
both, but may not he who has not leisure to be a
scholar find profit even in the lesser of the two,
if that only be attainable? Have I admitted that
one is the lesser? *O matre pulchra filia pulchrior*
is perhaps what I should say here.—*The Study of
Modern Languages.*

LOWELL ON THE GREEK AND THE MODERN DRAMA

Much of that merit of structure which is claimed
for the ancient tragedy is due, if I am not mistaken, to circumstances external to the drama itself,—to custom, to convention, to the exigencies

of the theatre. It is formal rather than organic.
The *Prometheus* seems to me one of the few Greek
tragedies in which the whole creation has developed itself in perfect proportion from one central germ of living conception. The motive of the
ancient drama is generally outside of it, while in
the modern (at least in the English) it is necessarily within. Goethe, in a thoughtful essay,
written many years later than his famous criticism
of Hamlet in *Wilhelm Meister,* says that the distinction between the two is the difference between
sollen and *wollen,* that is between *must* and *would.*
He means that in the Greek drama the catastrophe
is foreordained by an inexorable Destiny, while
the element of Freewill, and consequently of
choice, is the very axis of the modern. The definition is conveniently portable, but it has its limitations. Goethe's attention was too exclusively
fixed on the Fate tragedies of the Greeks, and upon
Shakespeare among the moderns. In the Spanish
drama, for example, custom, loyalty, honour, and
religion are as imperative and inevitable as doom.
In the *Antigone,* on the other hand, the crisis lies
in the character of the protagonist. In this sense
it is modern, and is the first example of true char-
acter-painting in tragedy. But, from whatever
cause, that exquisite analysis of complex motives,
and the display of them in action and speech, which

constitute for us the abiding charm of fiction, were quite unknown to the ancients. They reached their height in Cervantes and Shakespeare, and, though on a lower plane, still belong to the upper region of art in Le Sage, Molière, and Fielding. The personages of the Greek tragedy seem to be commonly rather types than individuals. In the modern tragedy, certainly in the four greatest of Shakespeare's tragedies, there is still something very like Destiny, only the place of it is changed. It is no longer above man, but in him; yet the catastrophe is as sternly foredoomed in the characters of Lear, Othello, Macbeth, and Hamlet as it could be by an infallible oracle. In *Macbeth,* indeed, the Weird Sisters introduce an element very like Fate; but generally it may be said that with the Greeks the character is involved in the action, while with Shakespeare the action is evolved from the character. In the one case, the motive of the play controls the personages; in the other, the chief personages are in themselves the motive to which all else is subsidiary.—*Shakespeare Once More.*

WHAT IS A CLASSIC?

GOETHE'S ANSWER

He who considers it an indispensable duty, both in speaking and in writing, to make words express a definite meaning will very rarely use the expressions, "classic author" or "classic works." When and where originates a classic national author? When he finds in the history of his nation great events leading to happy, important and harmonious consequences; when his compatriots display elevation of character, and depth of sentiment, and show in their actions strength and consistency; when he himself, imbued with the national spirit, and relying on his innate genius, can fully sympathise with the past as he does the present; when he finds that his country has reached so high a degree of culture that his own strides towards self-improvement become easy; when he has gathered together much and varied material, and profits by the efforts of his predecessors, successful or unsuccessful, and when in short, there exists such a conjunction of outward as well as inward conditions that his path becomes comparatively easy, so that he may in the best

years of his life plan and arrange and execute a
great work that befits his nature. . . .

An important piece of writing, like an important speech, is dictated by life itself; neither the
author nor the man of action is able to control
the circumstances under which he is born and under which he must live and work.   Even the greatest genius suffers in some respects from the defects
of his age, just as in other respects he profits from
its advantages, and an admirable national writer
is what the nation makes him. . . .

Unskilful critics do not see how fortunate young
men of talent nowadays are in arriving earlier at
a certain stage of development than was formerly
possible, and in acquiring a pure style adapted to
the subject.   To whom are they indebted for all
this if not to their predecessors, who in the last
half of the century, with incessant effort and
against many an obstacle, developed their abilities,
each in his own way?   Thus was created, one
might say, an invisible school, and a young man
who profits by its instruction enters a much larger
and more enlightened circle than the author of the
former day, whose uncertain steps were guided by
a dim light, until he himself gradually, and as it
were accidentally, saw his way into a larger sphere
of activity.   The half-critic, who would show us
the road by the flicker of his little lamp, arrives

much too late; the day has dawned, and we shall not again let down the shutters.—*On Literary Lawlessness* (*Literarischer Sanscüllotismus*), 1795.

SAINTE-BEUVE'S ANSWER

The best definition is an example. After France possessed her age of Louis XIV and was able to look upon it from some distance, she knew what it was to be a classic, better than any argument could have told her. The eighteenth century in all its confusion confirmed this conviction through a few beautiful works which came from its four great men. Read Voltaire's *Age of Louis XIV*, Montesquieu's *Greatness and Decline of the Romans*, Buffon's *Epochs of Nature*, the *Savoyard Vicar* and the beautiful reveries and descriptions of nature by Jean Jacques, and say whether the eighteenth century did not, in these memorable passages, succeed in reconciling tradition with independence and freedom of development. . . .

A true classic, as I should like to hear it defined, is an author who has enriched the human mind, who has really added to its treasures, who has carried it a step forward, who has discovered some unmistakable moral truth, or who has seized again upon some eternal passion of the human heart, and explored anew what seemed to be fully known; who has clothed his thought, his observation, or his discovery, no matter in what form, but in such a manner that the whole is large and impressive, delicate and sensible, sane and beautiful; who has spoken to all in a style of his own, which is at the same time that of all the world, in a style that is new without being newfangled, new and yet ancient, and easily at home in the language of all the ages.—*Causeries du Lundi,* Vol. III, *"Qu'est-ce qu'un Classique?"*

LOWELL'S ANSWER

The revival of letters, as it is called, was at first the revival of *ancient* letters, which, while it made men pedants, could do very little towards making them poets, much less towards making them original writers. There was nothing left of the freshness, vivacity, invention, and careless faith in the present which make many of the productions of the Norman Trouvères delightful reading even now. The whole of Europe during the fifteenth century produced no book which has continued readable, or has become in any sense of the word a classic. I do not mean that that century has left us no illustrious names, that it was not enriched with some august intellects who kept alive the apostolic succession of thought and spec-

ulation, who passed along the still unextinguished
torch of intelligence, the *lampada vitæ*, to those
who came after them.   But a classic is properly a
book which maintains itself by virtue of that happy
coalescence of matter and style, that innate and
exquisite sympathy between the thought that gives
life and the form that consents to every mood of
grace and dignity, which can be simple without being vulgar, elevated without being distant, and
which is something neither ancient nor modern, always new and incapable of growing old.   It is not
his Latin which makes Horace cosmopolitan, nor
can Béranger's French prevent his becoming so.
No hedge of language however thorny, no dragon-
coil of centuries, will keep men away from these
true apples of the Hesperides if once they have
caught sight or scent of them.   If poems die, it is
because there was never true life in them, that is,
that true poetic vitality which no depth of thought,
no airiness of fancy, no sincerity of feeling, can
singly communicate, but which leaps throbbing at
touch of that shaping faculty, the imagination.
Take Aristotle's ethics, the scholastic philosophy,
the theology of Aquinas, the Ptolemaic system of
astronomy, the small politics of a provincial city
of the Middle Ages, mix in at will Grecian, Roman,
and Christian mythology, and tell me what chance
there is to make an immortal poem of such an in-

congruous mixture. Can these dry bones live?
Yes, Dante can create such a soul under these ribs
of death that one hundred and fifty editions of his
poem shall be called for in these last sixty years,
the first half of the sixth century since his death.
Accordingly I am apt to believe that the com-
plaints one sometimes hears of the neglect of our
older literature are the regrets of archæologists
rather than of critics. One does not need to ad-
vertise the squirrels where the nut-trees are, nor
could any amount of lecturing persuade them to
spend their teeth on a hollow nut.—*Essay on
Spenser.*

PHILOSOPHY AND RELIGION

GOETHE ON LAVATER

THE conception of humanity which he (Lavater) had evolved, in his own way and as the result of his own nature, was so closely related to the vivid idea of Christ he cherished in his heart that it seemed inconceivable to him how any one could live and breathe without being a Christian. My own relation to the Christian religion was merely a matter of sense and sentiment, and I had not the slightest conception of that physical affinity to which Lavater inclined. I was therefore greatly displeased by the passionate way in which a man so richly endowed as to mind and heart importuned me, as well as Mendelssohn and others, maintaining that we must either become Christians, that is to say Christians according to his fashion, or convert him to our views, and convince him of the truth of that in which we had found peace of mind. This demand, so directly opposed to that liberal view of humanity which I had gradually acquired, produced anything but a good effect on me. All unsuccessful efforts at proselytising merely result in making him whom we would

convert more rigid and obstinate than ever. Such
proved to be my case, all the more so as Lavater
finally put before us the painful dilemma:
"Either Christian or Atheist!"   Thereupon I declared that if he would not leave me the Christianity I had hitherto cherished, I could easily
decide for atheism, all the more so as no one knew
exactly what was meant by either.—*Autobiography*, Part III, Book XIV.

GOETHE ON SPINOZA

I

I had not wholly neglected to cultivate the philosophic side of my nature, and had to some extent
appropriated the thoughts and the method of a
very extraordinary man, and, hasty as my study
of him had been, I was already conscious of his
important influence upon my mind. This great
thinker, who was destined to give a new direction
to my philosophical outlook upon the world, was
Spinoza. After having vainly cast about me for
something that might answer my peculiar mental
requirements, I at last happened upon his *Ethics*.
I could not easily give an account of what I read
in this work, or perhaps read into it; suffice it to
say that I found in it a sedative for my passions,
and that it opened to me a wide view of the realm
of perception and morals. What drew me espe-

cially towards him was the utter unselfishness which shone forth in his every sentence. Those strange words: "He who truly loves God must not ask that God love him in return," and all the premises on which they rest, as well as their logical consequences, filled my whole mind. To be unselfish in everything, most of all in love and friendship, was my greatest desire, my maxim and my practice. My own words, impertinently used later on: "If I love thee, is it thine affair?" show what I felt at the time. However, it must not be forgotten that the closest unions are those of opposites. Spinoza's conciliatory and reposeful nature was in striking contrast to my restless activity, his mathematical method was the direct opposite of my poetic way of thinking and writing; and his very precision, which some thought ill adapted to ethical subjects, made me his enthusiastic disciple and most thorough-going admirer. Mind and heart, reason and sentiment, were all drawn to him by inevitable affinity, and thus two entirely different natures became closely united.—*Autobiography*, Part III, Book XIV.

II

I had not thought of Spinoza for a long time, and now I was led to take up his works again through a diatribe against him. I found in our library a little book, the author of which violently attacked that original thinker. In order to add zest to the warfare he had inserted as a frontispiece a picture of Spinoza with the inscription: *Signum reprobationis in vultu gerens*, meaning thereby that he bore the imprint of depravity on his face. There was no denying that such was the case, on looking at the engraving, which was perfectly wretched and a ghastly caricature. I was reminded by it of the practices of those combatants in literary warfare who first utterly misrepresent their adversaries and then attack them as monsters of iniquity.

The little book, however, made no impression upon me, for I am not fond of controversies, preferring, indeed, to learn what the author himself thinks, rather than hear from some one else how he ought to have thought. Still, curiosity led me to turn to the article "Spinoza" in Bayle's Dictionary, a work as valuable and useful for its learning and acuteness as it is ridiculous and pernicious because of its tedious gossip.

The article on Spinoza excited my displeasure and distrust. The man is, first of all, represented as an atheist and his opinions as despicable; but immediately afterwards we are told that he was a quiet thinker, immersed in his studies, a good citizen, communicative and peaceable. The writer seemed to have quite forgotten the words of the gospel: *"By their fruits ye shall know them."* For how could a life pleasing to God and man result from corrupt principles?

I well remember what peace of mind and clearness of ideas took possession of me when I first turned over the pages of the posthumous works of that remarkable man. I could still recall the effect itself, though the particulars had escaped me; I rushed once more to take up the books to which I owed so much, and again they spoke to me in the same accents of peace. I read and read on, and thought, as I analysed my feelings, that I had never before looked at the world with such clear vision.—*Autobiography*, Part IV, Book XVI.

GOETHE ON THE BIBLE

While the study of German antiquities, partly from a natural fondness, partly for literary purposes, possessed my mind, I was from time to time turned aside from it by my biblical researches and religious sympathies: for the life and deeds of Luther, which shed their lustre on the sixteenth century, again and again led me back to the Holy Scriptures and to the consideration of religious sentiments and opinions. It flattered my petty

self-esteem to look upon the Bible as a work gradually compiled by various hands and corrected at
different periods—a view then by no means prev-
alent and far from being accepted in the circle
in which I moved. As regards the deeper meaning, I adhered to Luther's version, while as regards details I had recourse to Schmid's liberal
translation, making use, as far as possible, of the
little Hebrew I knew. That there are contradictions in the Bible no one nowadays denies. Speaking generally, an effort was made to reconcile
these contradictions by using the clearest passages
as the basis of interpretation, and approximating
to it, as far as possible, those that were contradictory and less clear. My desire, however, was to
find out by close examination which passage expressed best the obvious meaning; this I considered authoritative and the others I rejected as in-
terpolated. For at that time already I had gained
a deeply grounded conviction, concerning which
I am unable to say whether it was the result of
my own reflection, or had been suggested or inspired by others. It was to this effect: In everything handed down to us, especially in writing, the
all-important point is the inner meaning, the pur-
port and tendency of the work; herein lies the
fundamental value, that which is divine and effective, and remains intact and indestructible.

Neither time nor external influences of whatever kind can affect this inner spirit, any more than bodily sickness can affect the healthy mind. Thus language, dialect, peculiarities of style, and the diction itself are to be regarded as the body of every intellectual work, and this body, though closely akin to the inner spirit, is exposed to deterioration and decay. Indeed, no tradition can, from its very nature, be handed down in all its purity, nor if it were to come down to us, could it be fully understood in the course of time. The insufficiency of the means by which such traditions are handed down militates against the preservation of their purity; differences in time and place, and especially in human capacity and ways of thinking, prevent their being understood by later generations; and therefore interpreters can never agree as to the meaning of such traditions.

Hence we ought to make it our duty to search out the essence and real nature of any book that particularly interests us, to look upon it in its relations to our inner self, and above all to consider to what extent that which is vital in it will act upon and promote our own vitality. What is purely external and without influence upon us, or that which is subject to doubt, may be left to the critics who, even if they are able to cut up the whole into fragments, will never succeed in robbing us of the foundation on which we firmly stand, or in shaking for a moment the confidence which we have once for all acquired.

This conviction, born of faith and experience, which serves and strengthens us in the most important emergencies, forms the basis of the structure of my life, both in its ethical and literary aspect. It is, as it were, a safe and highly remunerative investment, even though, in single cases, it may be used with poor judgment. Looked at in this way, the Bible disclosed its real meaning to me. I had, as is customary in the religious instruction of Protestants, gone through it several times in a perfunctory way, indeed had familiarised myself with it by fits and starts, going forward and backward. The blunt naturalness of the Old Testament and the tender naïveté of the New had attracted me in parts, but in their entirety they had never fully appealed to me. Now, however, the diverse character of the various books no longer perplexed me, and their significance and sequence became perfectly clear to my mind. Indeed the book had captivated my feelings to such an extent that I never more could do without it. It was this emotional side that rendered me proof against all scoffers, whose dishonesty was apparent to me at a glance. I not only despised these, but became perfectly furious at

them, and I remember in particular that in my
childish fanaticism I felt like strangling Voltaire
for his *Saul,* had I been able to lay hands on
him. Any kind of honest investigation, on the
other hand, I keenly enjoyed; the revelations concerning Oriental localities and modes of dress,
which enlightened the public more and more, I
hailed with the greatest pleasure, and thus continued to exercise my ingenuity in the study of
these cherished traditions.

The reader is aware that at an earlier period
I had tried to picture to myself the conditions of
a primeval world, as described in the first book
of Moses. Bent on proceeding in an orderly fashion, step by step, I now took up, after a long in-
terruption, the second book. But how great the
difference! In proportion as my child-like exuberance had vanished, I found an enormous gap
opening between the second book and the first.
The complete break with the past is expressed in
the few significant words: "Now there arose a
new king over Egypt, which knew not Joseph."
But the people likewise, unnumbered as the stars
of Heaven, had almost forgotten the ancestor to
whom Jehovah, under the starry heavens, had
made the very promise that was now fulfilled. I
plodded through the five books with incredible
trouble, with insufficient ability and equipment,

and in so doing hit upon the strangest ideas. I had discovered that it was not the ten commandments that were written upon the tables of law; that the Israelites had not wandered forty years, but only a short time, through the desert, and I furthermore imagined that I was able to throw an entirely new light on the character of Moses.

Even the New Testament was not safe from my inquiries, and I did not shrink from applying to it my analytical spirit, although my affection for it led me to agree with the wholesome saying, Let the evangelists contradict each other, as long as the gospel does not contradict itself. In this field also I thought I had made all sorts of discoveries. The gift of tongues, imparted at the feast of Pentecost with such vivid splendour, I interpreted in a rather abstruse manner, which was not apt to gain many adherents.—*Autobiography*, Part III, Book XII.

GRILLPARZER ON RELIGIOUS ANTAGONISMS

When once the spirit of investigation has become universal, it will not easily set barriers to itself, least of all will it allow arbitrary outside interference to interpose them. Reason is quite willing to admit that there are some riddles it cannot solve, and it recognises as a benefit any bridging of the gulf it cannot cross, but only in so far as what is offered is not opposed to its very essence, and commands respect in itself. Nevermore, however, will reason tolerate any interference on the part of tradition with the established laws of Nature and the foundations of moral order. Creation out of nothing, transubstantiation, original sin, and redemption through merit other than our own will probably never again be seriously discussed. But all this may long survive in a sort of mysterious indefiniteness, and by reason of its moral value Christianity may—indeed, let us hope it will—continue to accompany mankind to the end. No power on earth, however, will succeed in reviving religious antagonisms. These cannot be forcibly brought back into modern life; any attempt in this direction would result in their dissolving into their real nothingness.*

GRILLPARZER ON HEGEL

The harm that Hegel's philosophy has done to German culture may perhaps be summarised as follows: First of all, he has through his speculations, which brooked no contradiction, suppressed the natural expression of thought—that which is ordinarily called common-sense. Secondly, his philosophy, by its obscurity, nay unintelligibility, has reared blind followers, who make themselves heard everywhere. And by its assurance that the world has now become transparent, and that the riddle of the universe has been solved, his philosophy has bred a self-conceit the like of which never existed before.*

GOETHE ON LITERATURE AS INFLUENCED BY SURROUNDINGS

Schiller, it is true, was quite young when he wrote his *Robbers,* his *Love and Intrigue,* and his *Fiesco,* but, to be honest, all these plays are rather manifestations of an extraordinary talent than proof of the mature intellect of the author. Schiller, however, is not to blame for this, but rather the existing cultural condition of Germany and the great difficulty which we all experience in striking out upon new paths.

Take Béranger, who can teach us quite a different lesson. He is the son of poor parents, the descendant of a poor tailor; starting as a petty printer's apprentice, he obtains a position in some office at a small salary; he has never been to a high-school or a university, and yet his songs show a mature and cultivated intellect; they are full of grace, of wit, and the most delicate irony, and his language is so perfect that he has the admiration not only of France, but of all civilised Europe.

Now imagine this same Béranger, instead of being born and brought up in a metropolis like Paris, as the son of a poor tailor in Jena or Weimar, and let him continue his life in these little places, cramped and miserable, and ask yourself what fruit the same tree, grown in such a soil and in such an atmosphere, would have borne.

We admire the tragedies of the ancient Greeks, but if we view the matter in the proper light we ought to admire, rather, the age and the nation; yet, in comparing them carefully, we find that these plays show certain differences, and though one poet may seem somewhat greater and more perfect than another, still, taking them together, all the plays have the same general character. It is the character of grandeur, of fitness, of sanity, of the humanly perfect, of great wisdom and lofty thought, of pure intuition, and many other qualities that might be mentioned. When we find all these qualities, not only in the dramatic works that have come down to us, but also in Greek lyrics and epics, in Greek philosophers, orators, and historians, and, in equally high degree, in the surviving works of plastic art, we must arrive at the conviction that these qualities were not merely characteristic of individuals, but were the common property of the nation and the entire age.

Now take Burns; is he not great because the old songs of his ancestors lived in the mouths of the people, because they were sung to him in his cradle, because he grew up among them as a boy, and because the great excellence of these examples became a part of his very being, so that his poetry proceeded from a living basis? And was not, moreover, his greatness due to the fact that his own songs instantly fell upon receptive ears, that they greeted him in the field, sung by reapers and girls bending over the sheaves; and that they welcomed him in the inn, sung by merry boon-companions? It was easy enough to succeed amid such surroundings.—*Eckermann's Conversations with Goethe.*

LESSONS FROM THE MASTERS

THE value of the lessons taught us by the eminent critics we are considering would be largely lost if we failed to see their bearing on the literary questions of the day. The critical faculty is commonly supposed to be antagonistic to creative ability; but in Goethe, Grillparzer, and Lowell we find the productive as well as the critical faculty equally manifest. In the case of Sainte-Beuve the prodigious mass of his critical work outweighs in importance even his uniquely valuable *History of Port-Royal*. It is rare indeed to find the analytic gift joined to such fruitful activity as characterised the lives of Goethe, Grillparzer, Sainte-Beuve, and Lowell. It was their incessant and passionate endeavour to hold up to their countrymen the great models of foreign literatures, in order to bring home to them the excellence of their own great writers. Their chosen field was the universal realm of thought and beauty. Imbued with reverence for classic ideals, they are equally inspired by the wisdom of the East; they seek what is admirable in German, French, Spanish and Italian literature, and turn aside to gather flowers from the literary bypaths

295

of other nations. Their sympathetic ken embraced all great works that have stood the test of time; and they passed by the mediocre and ignoble, regardless of the insistence of contemporary clamour. They never wrote or spoke to please the crowd, but always to satisfy their literary conscience; they appealed only to the cultivated taste of the mature and receptive. Grillparzer's solitary critical jottings during so many years bear the same note of sincerity and fulness of knowledge as Goethe's discursive talks with his scholarly intimates, Lowell's elaborate reviews, or Sainte-Beuve's Monday *Causeries,* which, with apparently conversational ease, were addressed to all literary Paris. Though the American critic was far more prodigal of recondite lore than the German, Austrian and French, all four possessed a wholesome dread of pedantry, and they never criticised in order to demonstrate their own superior wisdom. They bore in mind Lessing's warning: "A writer of note will not write merely to show his wit and scholarship; he addresses himself to the best and most enlightened of his time and deigns to write only what may please them or what will affect their feelings." In this aspect the critical work of Goethe, Grillparzer, Sainte-Beuve and Lowell is identical, however different in form and expression.

No critic has condemned more severely than Goethe the empty parade of knowledge. "Some books," he said, "seem to have been written not for the purpose of teaching us something, but to let us know that the author knew something," and as for the limitations of the critic, he remarked: "Rightly considered we learn only from books which are beyond our ability to criticise. The author of a book which we can criticise would have to learn from us." But no one has spoken with greater emphasis than Goethe upon the importance of constantly adding to our knowledge if we would rightly judge literature and life. "Talent of every kind," he said to Eckermann, "is fed by knowledge, and only through it can it exercise its strength." He said of himself to Chancellor Müller, in 1830: "Would it have been worth my while to live to the age of eighty if I had always thought the same thoughts? I strive to think every day of something different, something new, in order not to get stale. One must change incessantly, and renew and rejuvenate himself, in order not to become rigid."

In the steady pursuit of wisdom all the greatest geniuses attained their perfection. Young talents, conscious of their power, shrink from the slow process of weeding and pruning with which even genius in its prime cannot dispense. Ve-

hemence of assertion is a natural concomitant of
youth, but recognition of this fact does not absolve
the critic from the duty of pointing out to gifted
minds the value of moderation and self-discipline.
It is well known how Goethe, after emerging from
the period of his own youthful turbulence, recoiled
from the seething spirit of Schiller's *Robbers*.
He speaks of Schiller's powerful but immature
talent which had "flooded the country with a torrent of moral and dramatic paradoxes."

The period of Schiller's intellectual lawlessness
was brief and perhaps a necessary condition of
the development of his genius. In the case of so
many writers of the day who defy tradition and
set up standards of their own, lawlessness is the
only law of their being. No growth is possible,
because the seed is lacking. They start with deliberate ignorance and deceitful paradox, and end
where they began. The current insistence on the
right of the individual to cultivate his talent in his
own way deceives only the ignorant. Individual
liberty of this kind can result only in collective en-
slavement. "You will find," said Goethe, speaking of art, "that every great master has used what
was excellent in his predecessors, and this fact has
made him great. Men like Raphael do not grow
spontaneously. They had their root in the great
works of antiquity. Had they not made use of

the advantages open to them, there would be little
to say about them.'' What is true of art is equally
true of literature. The restlessness of modern
endeavour in literature and art, call it by whatever name we please, betokens only weakness.
We are invited to call the bewildering change progress, but for one genius who creates something
original there are a thousand blunderers, who, in
attempting to throw discredit on the old, merely
demonstrate the hopelessness of the new. ''To
make innovations,'' says Lessing, ''may be the
characteristic of a great mind or a small one. The
great discards the old because it has been found
insufficient or false, the small because it is old.
While the former is influenced by reason, the latter is by disgust. Genius wants to do more than
its predecessor, he who apes genius, merely something different.'' And Goethe wrote: ''There is
no more stupid error than the belief of talented
young people that they lose all credit for originality by admitting the truth of that which has already been recognised as such by others.''
''There is constant talk about originality,'' he said
to Eckermann, ''but what does it mean? As soon
as we are born the world around us begins to act
upon us, and so it goes on until the end. And,
after all, what can we call our own but our energy,
strength and determination. If I could recount

all I owe to my great predecessors and contemporaries there would be little left indeed that I could call my own.''

It is not easy to realise how much harm is done by the complaisant *laudator temporis præsentis* who decries all attempts of serious critics to set bounds to the ambition of young aspirants to literary laurels. It has indeed always been an ungrateful task to check immature exuberance. Lessing wrote: ''We have now a school of critics whose chief criticism consists in throwing suspicion on all criticism. 'Genius, genius,' they repeat endlessly. 'Genius disregards all rules. What genius creates becomes the rule.' Thus they flatter genius—in my opinion—in order that they may be regarded as geniuses themselves. But they show too clearly that they have not a spark of it themselves when they add in the same breath: 'Rules stifle genius.' As if genius could be suppressed by any power in the world! . . . Not every critic is a genius, but every genius is a born critic. Genius proves its own rules.''

The public cannot be argued into mistaking mediocrity for genius, nor does it long mistake genius for mediocrity. But the effect of the so-called kindly critic on mediocre authors is disastrous. He not only encourages feeble effort, but literally calls it into being. Dozens of young authors

spring into existence and find publishers because
dozens of others have written before them, who,
thanks to the plaudits of undiscriminating critics
and the thoughtlessness of undiscriminating readers, achieved a fleeting notoriety. It is a misfortune to any country to have its literary taste de-
bauched by critical arbiters who have so little
equipment for their calling. France, having for
centuries cherished veneration for literary genius,
has perhaps set the world the best example of an
almost unbroken line of critical authorities, of
whom Sainte-Beuve, in the recent past, was merely
the foremost representative.

The trite warning to the sceptical critic to look
out for unrecognised genius need scarcely be
met by the obvious observation that unmistakable
genius cannot be mistaken, and that even striking
talent is quick to find recognition. Witness the
rapidity, in our own time, with which the fame of a
Kipling, Rostand, Maeterlinck and Anatole France
has spread. Nor is it profitable, in the case of contemporaries, to raise the question of the difference between genius and talent. Posterity alone,
that is to say, the best international judgment, in
the ripeness of time, can assign to creative force
its definite rank. Grillparzer, referring to the extravagant claims made for the lawless genius
we all so well know, penned the lines: ''Denn das

Genie, es laüft in allen Gassen, doch seltener als je
ist das Talent.'' (Genius indeed may be met with
at every street corner, but talent is scarcer than
ever.) Goethe has said the final word on the subject in his remark:

"What is genius but the power of doing deeds
that can stand before God and Nature, of producing permanent results? All of Mozart's works
are of this kind; there is in them a productive
power which acts upon generation after generation, and it will be many a day before that is exhausted. This is equally the case with other great
composers and with all great artists. How potent
has been the influence upon succeeding centuries
of Phidias and Raphael, of Dürer, and Holbein!
He who first invented the forms and proportions
of Old-German architecture, which in the course of
time made possible the Strassburg Minster and the
Cologne Cathedral, was likewise a genius; for his
thought has retained its productive power to this
day and still exerts its influence. Luther was a
very formidable genius. His influence has lasted
many a day, and we cannot foretell how many centuries may elapse before he will cease to be productive. Lessing disclaimed the lofty title of
genius, but his permanent influence tells against
his disclaimer. There are in literature, on the
other hand, other great names who during their

lifetime were considered great geniuses, but whose influence ceased with their life, and who therefore were less important than they and others thought.''

It is the crowning merit of the great international critics that they held their balance true. The recognition of talent never led them to overpraise its power, and as there can be no just criticism of others which is not based on the clear recognition of one's own limitations, so they saw clearly what they themselves could and could not do. Goethe gave a striking illustration of the wholly impersonal attitude of self-criticism in an oft-quoted remark concerning Tieck.

''Tieck,'' he said to Eckermann, ''is a man of great talent, and no one can be more sensible of his great merits than myself, but it is a mistake to raise him beyond his own height and place him on the same level with me. I can say so plainly, for it matters nothing to me, inasmuch as I have not made myself. I should act similarly if I compared myself with Shakespeare, who also did not make himself, but who is nevertheless a being of a higher order, to whom I look up with reverence.'' Now this just recognition of the limits of praise is precisely what distinguishes the true critic from his counterfeit. Every nation furnishes instances of this inability ''to see ourselves as others see us.''

In its worst manifestation it leads to blind chauvinism, and it is a national calamity if great literary talent lends its influence to this perversion of
the natural love of one's country. Rudyard Kipling is a conspicuous example of the harmful stimulus given to imperialistic ideas by seductive poetic appeals, those ideas which, in Edmund Gosse's
language, lead to "the isolation of the Anglo-
Saxon mind." It may be said without exaggeration that the recrudescence of the mediæval idea
according to which the interests of nations are always opposed to each other is fostered by the
thoughtless literary critic who magnifies the importance of the achievements of his own country. Self-glorification on the part of one nation
is certain to arouse self-glorification on the part
of another. It is to be regretted that even so eminent a critic as Hermann Grimm allowed himself
to speak of Goethe's *Faust* as "the greatest work
of the greatest poet of all times and all nations"
—a statement which we may well contrast with
Goethe's saner estimate of himself as compared
with Shakespeare.

As we turn the pages of the masters of criticism, and compare their ways of treating the subjects that interested them in common, we are
struck, above all, by their reverence for the past,
their deference to the great, their moderation and

modesty.   There is in them not a trace of the shallow piquancy, the elaborate paradox, the cynical self-complacency of the so-called brilliant critic of the day.   No country in the world needs the example of these sober, self-respecting and respectful men of letters more than ours, where the teachings of our own wise men of the past are in danger of being forgotten.   We shall, let us hope, again see the rise of literary genius among us, but we must beware lest we lose the standards by which genius is measured.   What avails all else if we lack discrimination and self-restraint?   "To miss decorum," says a recent thoughtful writer,[1] "is to become incapable of what is best in art and literature (not to speak of life itself); it is to lose the secret of selection and the grand manner."

To what else did the great critics owe their influence but to this "secret of selection"?   They heard the call of the present as we do, but they never exaggerated its claims, and they felt the need of going back, again and again, to the great masters who have permanently enriched the world. He who does not feel this need merely gives proof of his intellectual poverty.   Surely, what the wisest could not be without, lesser minds can ill afford to spare.   No one returned more constantly to the

[1] Professor Irving Babbitt, in an article on Diderot in *The Nation*.

perennial sources of inspiration than Goethe. To read a great writer or see a great picture was a constant incentive to read and see again. "Molière," he said to Eckermann, "is so great that he astonishes us anew every time we read him. He stands alone. . . . I read several of his plays every year, just as, from time to time, I look at engravings of pictures by the great Italian masters. For we small men are not able to preserve within us the greatness of such things, and must therefore return to them from time to time in order to refresh our impressions."

It is idle to imagine that literary genius can afford to go its own solitary way, scorning knowledge, and be the better for it. The gifted minds may select their own manner of observing and studying, but observe and study they must, and ignorance becomes them as ill as it does the average man. Matthew Arnold has well said: "Wordsworth cared little for books, and disparaged Goethe. I admire Wordsworth, as he is, so much that I cannot wish him different; and it is vain, no doubt, to imagine such a man different from what he is, to suppose that he *could* have been different. But surely the one thing wanting to make Wordsworth an even greater poet than he is—his thought richer, and his influence of wider application—was that he should have read

more books, among them, no doubt, those of that
Goethe whom he disparaged without reading
them.''

If we learned nothing else from the great writers, we could still profit by their serenity, which
is so lamentably absent from the writing of the
day.   They found pleasure in their work and they
gave pleasure to the reader.   The master dramatists wrote no problem plays, the master novelists
no pathological novels, the master poets no morbid
poetry, though they too knew something of the
problems of mankind and the evils of society.
Goethe, Grillparzer, Sainte-Beuve and Lowell,
with all their diversities of temper and character,
wrote in a serene spirit.   What they created and
what they strove for tended to make the world better and happier.   They had in common the trait
which, as Emerson says, ''properly belongs to the
poet.   I mean his cheerfulness, without which no
man can be a poet, for beauty is his aim. . . . The
true bards have been noted for their firm and
cheerful temper.''   Indeed, the practice of all
great critics shows that cheerfulness is an important part of their creed.   The serene atmosphere which pervades the writings of Goethe,
Grillparzer, Sainte-Beuve, and Lowell is the result of an inner enthusiasm for what is beautiful
and excellent, and enthusiasm is incompatible

with a cynical spirit. Our modern brood of melancholy, formless, paradoxical and insincere writers would have been intolerable to these critics, with their keen detestation of sham. There were unhappy poets in those days as well, but who reads them to-day? "All the poets," says Goethe, "write as if they were ill and the whole world a hospital. They all speak of the woes and the miseries of this earth and of the joys of a hereafter; all are dissatisfied. . . . This is a real abuse of poetry, which was given to us to hide the petty discords of life and to make man contented with the world and with his condition."

Lowell, in a passage full of whimsical wisdom, enforces the lesson of cheerfulness in modern life. His good humour smiles through his very doubts. "It is noteworthy that literature, as it becomes more modern, becomes also more melancholy, and that he who keeps most constantly to the minor key of hopelessness, or strikes the deepest note of despair, is surest of at least momentary acclaim. Nay, do not some sources of happiness flow less full or cease to flow as settlement and sanitation advance, even as the feeders of our streams are dried by the massacre of our forests? We cannot have a new boulevard in Florence unless at sacrifice of those ancient city-walls in which inspiring memories had for so many ages

built their nests and reared their broods of song.
Did not the plague, brooded and hatched in those
smotherers of fresh air, the slits that thorough-
fared the older town, give us the *Decameron?*
And was the price too high? We cannot widen
and ventilate the streets of Rome without grievous
wrong to the city that we loved, and yet it is well
to remember that this city too had built itself out
of and upon the ruins of that nobler Rome which
gave it all the wizard hold it had on our imagination. The Social Science Congress rejoices in
changes that bring tears to the eyes of the painter
and the poet.   Alas! we cannot have a world made
expressly for Mr. Ruskin, nor keep it if we could,
more's the pity! Are we to confess, then, that
the world grows less lovable as it grows more convenient and comfortable? that beauty flees before
the step of the Social Reformer as the wild pen-
sioners of Nature before the pioneers? that the
lion will lie down with the lamb sooner than picturesqueness with health and prosperity? Morally, no doubt, we are bound to consider the Greatest Good of the Greatest Number, but there is
something in us, *vagula, blandula,* that refuses,
and rightly refuses, to be Benthamised; that asks
itself in a timid whisper, 'Is it so certain, then,
that the Greatest Good is also the Highest? and
has it been to the Greatest or to the Smallest Num-

ber that man has been most indebted?' For myself, while I admit, because I cannot help it, certain great and manifest improvements in the general well-being, I cannot stifle a suspicion that the
Modern Spirit, to whose tune we are marching so
cheerily, may have borrowed of the Pied Piper of
Hamelin the instrument whence he draws such be-
witching music.''

What chiefly repels the cautious observer of the
various manifestations of the modern spirit in literature is its vociferous positiveness and pretence.
The watchword "progress" covers a multitude of
reactionary sins. In the general rejection of the
standards of the past which we are told must give
place to the nameless wisdom of an unknown future, we simply go back to ancient barbarism.
The devotees of "naturalism" have wisely chosen
their designation. They have flung civilisation to
the winds and returned to the state of savage nature. Little do they reck or care what mankind
loses in the process.

How far have we wandered, in these days when
every literary aspirant insists on the righteous-
ness of his own gospel, from the example of the
great critics, whose whole activity showed that
they had no tolerance for the gospel of infallibility,
either in individuals or nations. "Let no one imagine," said the wise Goethe, "that the world has

been waiting for him as for a Messiah." Modern
literature is perpetually on the look-out for some
new prophet. Salvation is to come now from one
new preacher, now from another—the text does
not matter, so it be new and startling.

Can the world in the long run dispense with
simplicity and loveliness and lose the possessions
which make literature and life precious? "We
cannot yet afford," answers Emerson, "to drop
Homer, nor Æschylus, nor Plato, nor Aristotle,
nor Archimedes." Posterity will not side with
the modern critics who encourage the turbulent
lawlessness of the moderns; for praise of the ignoble is not only an offence against æsthetics, but
against the very order of society. Literary conscience concerns itself with deeper things than
novelty of theme and piquancy of treatment, and
the sense of beauty refuses to be satisfied with the
realistic search for the surface truth of things.
Goethe has said a beautiful word on this subject:

"Until recently the world believed in the hero-
ism of a Lucretia or of a Mucius Scævola, and this
belief inspired us with warmth and enthusiasm.
But now historical criticism tells us that those
heroes never lived and must be considered as
fables and fictions produced by the lofty imagination of the Romans. But of what use is such
paltry truth to us? If the Romans were great

enough to invent such heroes, we ought at least to be great enough to believe in them.''

It is this recognition of the power of the deeper truth, this seriousness of purpose, this perennial search for wisdom and loveliness, that made the master critics what they are.

THE END